DIGITAL CIVIL WAR

DIGITAL CIVIL WAR

CONFRONTING
THE FAR-RIGHT MENACE

PETER DAOU

MELVILLE HOUSE
BROOKLYN • LONDON

Digital Civil War
Copyright © 2019 by Peter Daou

First Melville House Printing: April 2019

Melville House Publishing

46 John Street
Brooklyn, NY 11201

and

Suite 2000
16/18 Woodford Rd.
London E7 0HA

mhpbooks.com
@melvillehouse

ISBN: 978-1-61219-787-6
ISBN: 978-1-61219-788-3 (eBook)

Designed by Euan Monaghan
Printed in the United States of America

10 9 8 7 6 5 4 3 2 1

A catalog record for this book is
available from the Library of Congress

For Z

CONTENTS

DIGITAL CIVIL WAR

FROM BEIRUT TO THE BELTWAY

———

War begins where reason ends.
—Frederick Douglass

On January 21, 2017, the day after Donald Trump's inauguration, women across America led the biggest single-day protest in U.S. history, marking the beginning of a movement that twenty-two months later swept Republicans out of their majority in the House of Representatives. The blue wave of 2018 put a dent in the GOP's political dominance and gave hope to millions of Americans that democracy was not lost. But in the early days of 2017, hope was in short supply for Democrats. A shell-shocked majority grappled with Hillary Clinton's electoral college defeat and with the looming prospect of minority white-nationalist rule. In that atmosphere of dread and despair, Virgin Group founder Richard Branson took to his company's website to share photos of a smiling Barack Obama kitesurfing at Branson's private Caribbean island. The pictures sparked a social media firestorm.

"What THE HELL #obama ! #kitesurf !!! Did you notice that the cheeto in chief #TRUMP is ruining my #America? GET BACK TO WORK MAN!!!" yelled Twitter user "Jon Snow." "Da Trumpstah," a commenter on the right-wing Breitbart News, sneered, "That smile says it all. i f'd over millions of Americans and they still love me." On Facebook, Nicholas McKenzie posted, "Fun day of kite surfing after 8 years of murdering civilians in the middle east . . . enjoy life." *New York Times* columnist Frank Bruni later wrote about "the robustness of Barack Obama's appetite for celebrity and luxury," arguing that Obama "gave unfettered vent to that once he left the White House and, in the months immediately thereafter, went yachting with Tom Hanks and Bruce Springsteen in Tahiti, kite surfing with Richard Branson in the Virgin Islands, rafting in Indonesia, golfing on the Scottish coast and biking under the Tuscan sun."[1]

Supporters quickly stepped up to defend the former president. "Barack Obama has GIVEN ENOUGH. He doesn't owe us a goddamn thing and it's not up to him to clean up this horrific mess. Let the man live. Let him kitesurf with moguls/make movies with Netflix/enjoy his life," tweeted writer Jennifer Boeder. "Love to see the smile on his face . . . the weight of the world has been lifted off his shoulders . . . Enjoying life as you should!! #ForeverMyPresident," Obama supporter Vicki Charlot wrote on Facebook. Journalist Brandon Gates tweeted, "Whether you disagree with his politics, or not, everyone should enjoy a vacation. Geez." On Reddit, "DarthRusty" wrote that if he were in Obama's position, "every picture taken of me by some paparazzi would have my middle finger fully extended." YouTube commenter "Julius Caesar" taunted Obama's detractors: "Just here to read all the comments from the butt hurt redneck Obama haters."

For online activists accustomed to a steady stream of vitriol, it was a typical day on the digital battlefield. But the Washington establishment was slow to grasp the breach in the body politic fueling these ferocious social media clashes. By 2018, however, mainstream pundits had begun to acknowledge what the online community had known for years—that traditional media narratives were no longer adequate to describe the severity of the red-blue split. Appearing on CNN, Watergate reporter Carl Bernstein declared that America was in a "cold civil war" and that Trump's bellicose rhetoric had brought it "to the point of ignition."[2] Bernstein's bleak assessment was echoed by NBC's Chuck Todd, who tweeted, "Let's be blunt, our political parties are waging a 'cold' civil war." *New York Times* columnist Thomas Friedman fretted, "I began my journalism career covering a civil war in Lebanon. I never thought I'd end my career covering a civil war in America."[3]

The fear that America is on the cusp of—or may already be embroiled in—some form of internecine war is well founded. On August 12, 2017, Heather Heyer, a thirty-two-year-old progressive activist, was mowed down by a white supremacist as she took part in a counterprotest against neo-Nazis in Charlottesville, Virginia. Earlier that summer, at a baseball field

121 miles from the site of Heyer's murder, a domestic abuser who belonged to a Facebook group called "Terminate the Republican Party" opened fire on Republican lawmakers practicing for the annual Congressional Baseball Game, wounding four people.

In a violent October 2018, the neo-fascist gang Proud Boys clashed with the anti-fascist group Antifa in Portland and New York City. Cell-phone video of the Manhattan melee showed a group of Proud Boys shouting slurs as they swarmed and stomped two victims. The *New York Times* reported that members of the group were seen "exulting about 'smashing' the head of a 'foreigner.'"[4] Later that month, a Trump supporter who had attacked liberals on social media mailed improvised explosive devices to CNN, Barack Obama, Hillary Clinton, Joe Biden, and a number of other prominent Democrats and progressive donors, including billionaires Tom Steyer and George Soros.

As news of the mail bombs broke, author and commentator Jared Yates Sexton tweeted, "When I was reporting from Trump rallies his supporters were talking about murder and violent revolution. They talked about killing the exact people who were targeted today." Digital activist Kaitlin Byrd reacted to the news with a Twitter thread about the roots of right-wing violence. "Whether it is cheering the likes of Jesse James or riding through the night with bedsheets and torches or shooting doctors or firebombing churches or murdering 168 people for the sin of being in a federal building, these people and their goals have always been with us," Byrd wrote, arguing that the threat of violence was not random. "It is not isolated. It is not unpredictable. It is not unprecedented. It is the legacy of self-ishness and white supremacy that we refuse to challenge. And it will come for us until we confront it," she tweeted.

Right-wing media put their own spin on the story, claiming that the intercepted explosive devices were an elaborate Democratic hoax. Michael Savage—a radio host who once mocked veterans suffering from PTSD—proclaimed that it was "a high probability" the entire incident was "a false flag to gain sympathy for the Democrats" and "to get our minds off the hordes of illegal aliens approaching our southern border."[5] Right-wing radio personality Rush Limbaugh, whose angry anti-liberal rants have shaped the views of a generation of Republicans, asked, "What sense does it make for a con-servative Republican to gum up the works here by sending a bunch of bombs that are not gonna go off and that are gonna be discovered?"[6]

Gateway Pundit, an influential far-right website, crowed that mainstream reporters were "SO HOPING this story of faulty bombs would sway Trump voters to change behavior ten days before the midterm election. So you can imagine the liberal media's frustration when the North Carolina crowd began chanting, 'CNN sucks!' at last night's [Trump] rally. Sorry liberals. CNN still sucks and the liberal media is still a Democrat echo-chamber."[7] Donald Trump, Jr., Trump's eldest son, liked a tweet that blared, "BREAKING: WHITE POWDER

IN BOMBS NOT BIOLOGICAL OR DANGEROUS. LIKELY BABY POWDER."

But the only hoax was the false-flag claim itself. The accused mail bomber was a registered Republican and Trump fanatic who had reportedly told his former employer, "If I had complete autonomy none of these gays or these blacks would survive." Jonathan Albright, director of the Digital Forensics Initiative at Columbia's Tow Center, studied the suspect's social media feeds and found that he had posted a "paid crisis actor" meme about Parkland shooting survivor David Hogg at least fifty-nine times in forty-eight hours. Right-wing conspiracy-mongering had radicalized him.

Days before the mail-bombing suspect was arrested—and his propaganda-plastered van confiscated—a white male shot and killed two black people at a Kroger supermarket in Jeffersontown, Kentucky. Surveillance video from earlier in the day showed the gunman trying to enter a predominantly black church. A spokesperson for the Jeffersontown Police Department said the Kroger shooting appeared to be "motivated by hate."

Capping off a deadly October, an armed white male with a trail of anti-Semitic online rants walked into a synagogue in Pittsburgh, yelled "all Jews must die," and opened fire, killing and wounding seventeen people. Hours before the slaughter, he posted a chilling message on Gab, an extremist-friendly social network: "Screw your optics, I'm going in." Reacting to the wave of violence, *Washington Post* Global Opinions editor

Karen Attiah tweeted, "As I think on the #PittsburghShooting and the #KrogerShooting, I reflect on why so many people of color get upset at journalism that treat white supremacists, racists and Neo-nazis as silly little curiosities. Death and terrorism has always been a part of U.S. white supremacy."

Journalist Jill Filipovic tweeted that "hate is an ecosystem" and "what we're seeing now are a bunch of people all acting out of the same general worldview—right-wing white nationalism." Filipovic argued that Trump and his cohorts had created conditions that fostered violent extremism: "We have a president who suggests that there is a vast conspiracy to harm good Americans—by which he means white Americans . . . We also have a Republican Party that goes along with him, aiding in normalizing ideas that have always animated the right." Filipovic noted that "right-wing media has successfully fed into this narrative of white grievance" and that the resulting propaganda system "has helped to convince millions of people that they are the victims of an unholy alliance of liberals, globalists, and dangerous foreigners."

Journalist David Neiwert, who has written extensively about eliminationist rhetoric in politics, tweeted that "one side of the political aisle, and only one, appears intent on provoking a violent civil war in America. And it is the [Republican] party currently in power." He described "gangs of heavily armed right-wing thugs, largely outsiders from rural and exurban areas, invading liberal urban centers with the full intent of provoking violence." Neiwert added, "I hang out among the alt-righters and militiamen who populate that side and listen to them. They all are brimming with eagerness to beat the shit out of liberals, and they're prepared to kill if they deem it necessary."

Neiwert's reporting is supported by data from the Anti-Defamation League, which found that between 2007 and 2016, "approximately 74% of deaths caused by domestic extremists were at the hands of right-wing extremists, about 24% of the victims were killed by domestic Islamic extremists, and the remainder [2%] were killed by left-wing extremists."[8] The Government Accountability Office (GAO) reported that from September 12, 2001, to December 31, 2016, violent extremists in the U.S. caused 225 deaths, of which 106 were by the far right and 119 by radical Islamist extremists. The left accounted for none of the deaths tallied in the GAO report.[9] A *Washington Post* analysis of extremist violence between 2010 and 2017 found that "attackers motivated by right-wing political ideologies have committed dozens of shootings, bombings and other acts of violence, far more than any other category of domestic extremist."[10]

Right-wing extremism didn't begin with Donald Trump's presidency, nor will it end with it, but the Republican Party's lurch to the far right in the aftermath of the 2016 election has pushed red-blue tensions to the breaking point. Sarah Kendzior, an independent journalist and icon of the progressive resistance, wrote that under Trump and the Republican Party "checks and balances are nearly gone. The executive branch was long ago corrupted; the independent legislature neutered by a GOP majority nakedly seeking one-party rule."[11] Consumer advocacy group Public Citizen warned that "American democracy is unraveling before our very eyes."[12]

In *The Death of Truth: Notes on Falsehood in the Age of Trump*, author and literary critic Michiko Kakutani wrote that people "are losing a sense of shared reality."[13] That reality gap is a function of extreme polarization, where Democrats see the GOP as a corrupt and reactionary party answerable only to its megadonors, Fox News, and the National Rifle Association; and Republicans view the "Demo*rat*" Party (emphasis on "rat") as an imminent threat to the republic, trampling the rights of "real Americans," confiscating their guns, threatening their values, and curtailing their freedoms. An editorial in AmmoLand, a website serving the firearms industry, characterized the left-right split as a "modern-day civil war for America's soul." The authors, Roger J. Katz and Stephen L. D'Andrilli, argued that each side "holds resolutely to one of two irreconcilable, mutually incompatible positions, representing two polar opposite ideological strains within the American polity."[14]

These bitter divisions between red and blue Americans are rooted in unresolved disputes over race, values, and identity that have festered and periodically boiled over since the nation's founding. The cruelties of America's past—the atrocity of slavery, the Trail of Tears, the bloodletting of the Civil War—cast long shadows over the present. As they should. "To forget the dead would be akin to killing them a second time," Holocaust survivor Elie Wiesel wrote in his memoir *Night*.[15]

Our struggles are not new, but technology has altered and expanded the field of battle. In *LikeWar: The Weaponization of Social Media*, P. W. Singer and Emerson T. Brooking wrote, "From the world's most powerful nations to the pettiest flame war combatants, all of today's fighters have turned social media into a weapon in their own national and personal wars."[16] Journalist Thomas E. Ricks, an adviser on national security at New America, predicted that "a contemporary homeland conflict would likely self-compose with numerous dynamic factions organized by digital tools around ideological and affinity networks."[17]

Indeed, America is in the throes of a *digital* civil war, not a "cold" or "soft" one. It is waged with words and images designed to inflict psychological harm, to wreak havoc with rhetoric. The combatants—citizens, activists, journalists, politicians, coders, conspiracists, hackers, and trolls—use technology to network and communicate, to connect with allies and target foes. Logging on every day is entering a war zone, a gauntlet of verbal abuse, gaslighting, and harassment. The unrelenting toxicity of social media is a feature, not a bug, of digital warfare. And like all wars, the Digital Civil War has its villains and heroes, traitors and patriots, the memorialized and the invisibilized. I write their story not as a historian or political scientist, but as an eyewitness—a child conscript and survivor of civil war in the Middle East, and a digital strategist in two U.S. presidential campaign war rooms.

My journey from a real to a rhetorical battlefield began in

the shadow of Mount Lebanon, a steep range that snakes along the eastern shores of the Mediterranean and climbs ten thousand feet to a snow-crowned summit at Qurnat as Sawdā'—the black peak. In its foothills lies Beirut, the imperishable city, host to a procession of civilizations: Roman, Phoenician, Hellenistic, Byzantine, Arab, Ottoman. My family settled in Beirut when it was the "Paris of the Middle East," a stomping ground for jet-setters and bon vivants, the stuff of postcards and bucket lists. Like Beirutis before me, I learned that places of antiquity are bound by immutable laws, and seasons of unrest must follow seasons of tranquility. In 1975, my beach-filled boyhood went up in flames, engulfed by a civil war that spanned fifteen years and annihilated 150,000 lives.

The Lebanese Civil War was a binge of brutality that pit neighbor against neighbor, friend against friend, relative against relative. The country's religious diversity made it a sectarian tinderbox. Once first blood was shed, the carnage was immense. Thousands of civilians were slaughtered simply for being born of the wrong denomination. Powerless to stop the external chaos, people built internal defenses, walls of grit and grim determination. In the alchemy of terror, wounds were transformed into medals, suffering into honor. To survive was to suppress fear, silence self-doubt, smash the rearview mirror, and drive forward, ever forward. I did just that, and the momentum carried me across two continents and three careers, depositing me a quarter century later in the minefield of U.S. politics.

When I entered the political arena at the turn of the millennium, I recognized the anger and vengefulness I'd seen in Beirut. I knew the cycles of hope and hopelessness. Lulls. Flareups. Cease-fires. I recognized the distortion of truth and facts and the dehumanization of adversaries. All of it was familiar. The Lebanese Civil War had prepared me for America's Digital Civil War. And it taught me that in conflict life goes on for most citizens even as others are in mortal danger. Following stretches of heavy shelling in Beirut, schools would reopen, people would shop, work, play. Similarly, the Digital Civil War is conducted against the backdrop of ordinary life: jobs, chores, vacations, sports, movies. That disconnect can be deceiving, leading some political observers to minimize the severity of the red-blue divide. But while it is true that millions of Americans are disengaged from day-to-day partisan battles—nonvoters, the unaffiliated, the disillusioned—it is also the case that millions of others are engaged in a political and cultural struggle that ultimately affects us all.

If there is a risk of drawing overbroad conclusions from America's furious social media clashes, there is a *greater* danger of minimizing the threat to marginalized and vulnerable people who face life-and-death consequences from the policy outcomes of those fights. The chaos and crosscurrents of U.S. politics should not lull us into underestimating the gravity of the rupture between the two major parties. On issue after issue, polls reveal stark partisan divisions: A June 2018 Gallup poll found that 88 percent of Republicans had "very or mostly favorable views" of the NRA, while only 24 percent of Democrats felt the same.[18] A Reuters/Ipsos poll released in July 2018 found that only 10 percent of Republicans strongly agreed that Russia attempted to interfere in the 2016 election on behalf of Trump, while 58 percent of Democrats strongly agreed.[19] According to an October 2018 Pew Research Center survey, 76 percent of Democrats said abortion should be legal in all or most cases, while only 36 percent of Republicans said the same.[20] Another 2018 Pew Research poll found that a paltry 11 percent of Republicans considered climate change a "very big" problem, compared to 72 percent of Democrats.[21]

The question, then, is this: When both sides claim a monopoly on conscience, is moral clarity possible? Can we cut through the noise and chaos to determine which party is responsible for the assault on our norms and principles? In short: Who's right?

To answer that question is to navigate a morass of relativism and recrimination. The mainstream media offer little help. *Washington Post* editor Martin Baron described journalists as "independent arbiters of fact,"[22] yet reporters and pundits have repeatedly resorted to false equivalence in the face of radicalization and polarization, treating a racist's hate speech as one side of a coin and his detractor's rebuttal as the other, a politician's lies as no more censurable than the outrage over those lies. Hypersensitive to accusations of liberal bias, most news outlets retreat to the refuge of "both-siderism," blaming everyone equally—and thus, no one at all.

Norman Ornstein, resident scholar at the American Enterprise Institute, wrote presciently in 2014 that "insisting on equivalence as the mantra of mainstream journalism . . . leaves the average voter at sea, unable to identify and vote against those perpetrating the problem. The public is left with a deeper disdain for all politics and all politicians, and voters become more receptive to demagogues and those whose main qualification for office is that they have never served, won't compromise, and see everything in stark black-and-white terms."[23]

The failure of the mainstream media and political establishment to serve as a counterbalance to the dishonesty and hypocrisy poisoning American politics leaves just one major national institution to provide a moral compass for the country. But that institution, the judiciary, tilts increasingly to the right. Republicans have played a ruthlessly effective long game, stacking federal courts and muscling staunch right-wing jurists onto the Supreme Court. "The only real question is just how far right the court will move," historian Julian E. Zelizer wrote.[24]

The bracing reality is that there are no referees, no judges, no religious leaders, no revered public figures, philosophers, or teachers with the standing to censure those who make a mockery of common sense and common decency. It is our responsibility as citizens to find solid ethical ground from which to make sound political judgments. The first step is to dispel the illusion that hewing to the center is always the reasonable course of action. Author and professor Tayari Jones wrote eloquently that the "American fetishization of the moral middle is a misguided and dangerous cultural impulse. The middle is a point equidistant from two poles. That's it. There is nothing inherently virtuous about being neither here nor there . . . What is halfway between moral and immoral?"[25]

The next step is to acknowledge that polarization is asymmetric—Republicans, not Democrats, are becoming more extreme. Researchers from the Berkman Klein Center for Internet & Society at Harvard University and the Center for Civic Media at MIT analyzed "hyperlinking patterns, social media sharing patterns on Facebook and Twitter, and topic and language patterns in the content of the 1.25 million stories, published by 25,000 sources over the course of the [2016] election." Sharing their findings in *Columbia Journalism Review*, the researchers noted that "polarization was asymmetric" and that the right-wing media ecosystem was "an internally coherent, relatively insulated knowledge community, reinforcing the shared worldview of readers and shielding them from journalism that challenged it." They found that the "pro-Trump media sphere appears to have not only successfully set the agenda for the conservative media sphere, but also strongly influenced the broader media agenda."[26]

In 2014, Princeton political scientist Nolan McCarty summarized the findings of an in-depth report on polarization in the United States. A key takeaway: "Despite the widespread belief that both parties have moved to the extremes, the movement of the Republican Party to the right accounts for most of the divergence between the two parties."[27] Since the publication of that report in 2014, the Republican Party has moved even further to the right, embracing and mainstreaming extremist positions on an array of contentious issues. Aided by a well-oiled right-wing media machine delivering carefully crafted messages to Republican voters, the far right has seized control of the GOP agenda and fought to reshape American government in its own image.

This has given rise to an army of digital warriors, led by women, who are using social media to speak out, mobilize, raise awareness, fund raise, and campaign. For the voters and activists who powered the blue wave that swept the Democrats to a House majority in the 2018 midterms, the Digital Civil War is not just about opposing Donald Trump and the GOP but surviving the ever-present menace of right-wing extremism.

If the battles sound familiar—women taking on the patriarchy, people of color taking on white supremacists, the disenfranchised taking on oligarchs, immigrants taking on xenophobes—they are. The Digital Civil War is yet another reckoning with the forces of oppression and hate that have sought a stranglehold on America since its birth. In 1962, James Baldwin wrote, "Not everything that is faced can be changed, but nothing can be changed until it is faced."[28] More than a half century after Baldwin wrote those words, the nation is once again facing its demons: intolerance, bigotry, ignorance, racism, nativism, and misogyny.

There is no telling how this fight ends, but as John Stuart Mill wrote during another civil war, "As long as justice and injustice have not terminated their ever-renewing fight for ascendancy in the affairs of mankind, human beings must be willing, when need is, to do battle for the one against the other."[29] Simply put, right is right, wrong is wrong, and it is our duty to defend the former and reject the latter, even while acknowledging that the purest of intentions, the strongest of convictions, and the soundest of arguments may not always prevail.

ONE

BATTLE FOR IDENTITY: THE REAL AMERICAN

———

White Christian males losing their place in the social
order decided they'd do anything to save themselves, and to
heck with morality. They made a bargain with the devil in
full knowledge. So the real question is: What does it mean
to be an American today? Who are we, goddamit?
—Roger Cohen, *New York Times* op-ed

Politics is the competing stories we tell about our country, our history, our government, our community, and ourselves. Where our stories intersect, there is consensus; where they diverge, debate; where they clash, division. And when the villains in those stories are our fellow citizens, there is strife. Today, the stories being told by Democrats and Republicans are incompatible, spurring legitimate concerns about the health and stability of U.S. democracy.

The digital age has transformed our social interactions and reshaped our political process. We let the world know what we think, where we go, who we know. We share intimate details about our lives willingly—and often unwittingly. We are turned inside out, so that our private thoughts become our public face. In engaging online over our values and beliefs, we are participating in a battle of ideas and ideals, a Digital Civil War in which dueling stories about American identity and history vie for dominance. The Republican Party's story, the story of the "real American," begins in the heart of the rust belt.

I-78 cuts across Pennsylvania's midsection, a bucolic landscape dotted with picturesque farmhouses under big skies and billowing clouds—a Hopper painting come to life. The interstate grazes Allentown's southern tip as it runs 144 miles from Union Township in Lebanon County to the Hudson River. Ten miles off its eastern edge, along a road littered with boarded-up storefronts, a partially lit neon sign hangs over the faded green awning of the Westside Restaurant, a gritty diner that has served locals and out-of-towners for more than fifty years. On Sundays, Westside patrons walk up the street to the Church of the Blessed Sacrament, a Catholic parish founded in 1887, torn down in 1917, and rebuilt in 1919 to accommodate its growing congregation. In the pews, under the soft light from clerestory windows, friends and neighbors gather in prayer.

In this part of America, tradition is honored, hard work is respected, and Christian values are prized. By Christian values, I mean the "compassion, kindness, humility, gentleness and patience" of Colossians 3:12. And by "this part of America," I mean Manhattan's Upper West Side. The Church of the Blessed Sacrament is on Seventy-First Street between

Broadway and Columbus Avenue. The Westside Restaurant is two blocks down, on the northeast corner of Sixty-Ninth Street and Broadway.

Millionaires may be minted by the minute on Wall Street, but homelessness among New York City's public school-children is at record highs and more than a quarter of the city's children live in poverty. While hedge-fund hotshots scoop up eight-figure Billionaires' Row condos, millions of New Yorkers teeter on the edge of financial ruin, their cost of living among the highest in the country. Sky-high commercial rents have devastated mom-and-pop retailers. One by one, beloved Manhattan establishments have shuttered, victims of the creeping malignancy of obscene wealth, the predatory greed that has transformed the Big Apple into a monument to inequality.

The tale of economic hardship in New York is echoed in towns and cities along I-78. So why is it unusual for Manhattan to be depicted in the elegiac language reserved for the rust belt? Because no cultural myth is more pervasive, no dogma more entrenched, than that of the small-town white male being the quintessential or "real" American, and his struggles the only meaningful ones. "The United States holds whiteness as the unifying force. Here, for many people, the definition of 'Americanness' is color," explained author Toni Morrison.[1] Or, as suffragist Elizabeth Cady Stanton famously wrote to her friend Susan B. Anthony in 1859, "Confer on me, great angel, the glory of White manhood, so that henceforth I may feel unlimited freedom."[2]

The "real American" story is a toxic brew of populism, nativism, and white supremacy packaged by the GOP, distributed by right-wing media, imbibed by the Republican base, and regurgitated by the mainstream press. It holds that the authentic American is a flag-waving, churchgoing, gun-owning, pro-military, small-town, conservative, straight white male from the country's midsection, whose politics are motivated by unwavering and unimpeachable convictions, and whose noble suffering is ignored by godless liberals and coastal elites. In this omnipresent fiction, "real Americans" are paragons of virtue who stand firm against liberal usurpers determined to steal their guns, rights, money, land, and liberty.

The "real American" story is the thread that runs through virtually every partisan fight in U.S. politics. It maintains that the white working class has been shunned by the Democratic Party, patronized by the "liberal media," mocked by Hollywood, stifled by identity politics, smothered by political correctness, and oppressed by big government. And it purports to explain why white working-class voters saw a kindred spirit in a wealthy New York real estate developer with gilded toilets.

Pulitzer Prize–winning columnist Eugene Robinson called the "real American" story "the most offensive and corrosive idea in our politics today." He warned, "Don't you dare buy it. Republicans are cynically peddling this un-American conceit. 'Real Americans' elected and continue to support President Trump, they claim, in defiance of snooty 'coastal elites' who are hopelessly out of touch with the country. It's a total crock, and shame on those using it for political gain."[3] Journalist Jennifer Rubin, a staunch Trump critic (and once a favorite of the political right), argued that Trump and his Fox News advocates "have perpetrated the fraud that only they are the voice of 'the people,'" and that "elites" don't understand "real America." As Rubin explained, "That's what authoritarian regimes and their followers always say."[4]

The battle over American identity, and its manifestation in the myth of the "real American," is a major front in the Digital Civil War. On Twitter—ground zero of the war— digital activist Delilah Asterales (HawaiiDelilah) wrote, "We in blue states and on the coasts and in urban centers are as much REAL America as folks in red states. We're sick to death of being held hostage by folks in flyover country lamenting the loss of the bad old days & obstructing progress." ABC News political analyst Matthew Dowd tweeted, "I am so sick of people deciding who 'real Americans' are. Whether you live on the coasts, or in between, or in a big city or small town, or were born here or are an immigrant, or a christian, jew, muslim, hindu, or nada, black, brown, white or whatever, you are a real American." Tom Nichols, a professor at the U.S. Naval War College and influential member of the Never Trump movement, echoed Dowd's frustration: "For the love of God, don't tell me about what Trump's Real 'Muricans in the Heartland want. I know what they want: more government action, including money, delivered with a smile, inflated respect, and pity, earned or not."

On Facebook, former Naval Surface Warfare officer Sheila Scarborough wrote: "Hi. PSA. I'm a 22+ year Navy veteran. I'm also a moderate/liberal. Yeah, we exist. Kindly stop questioning my patriotism by calling me a 'mob' or a 'libtard' or 'not a real American.' If you want to thank me for my service, do me a favor & read the Constitution that I swore to defend." Patricia Buchanan, a California-based information technology analyst, tweeted, "That whole 'coastal elite' thing kills me. I was born and raised on the California coast, a dirt poor hillbilly; and I care about everyone even if it cost me a few more bucks in taxes because I want to give back."

Even the conservative *National Review* expressed skepticism of the "real American" story, publishing "The Myth of Flyover Country's 'Real America,'" an article by former executive editor of *American Hunter*, Frank Miniter. "Does the 'real America' view mean that small-business owners who are struggling, working almost every waking hour as they raise children in Los Angeles, New York City, or Miami, somehow aren't real Americans?" Miniter asked. "This Mayberry idealism may seem harmless, just a romantic look back to the old values expressed in Norman Rockwell paintings. But it's not harmless," he wrote.[5]

Historian Nell Irvin Painter explained that "being a real American often meant joining antiblack racism and seeing oneself as white against the blacks." In *The History of White People*, Painter wrote that slavery "made the inherent inferiority of black people a foundational belief, which nineteenth-century

Americans rarely disputed. Very few people believed that people of African descent belonged within the figure of *the* American." In this view, she noted, "'Southerner' meant white southerner; 'American' required whiteness."[6] It is in this context that we can understand the persistence of birtherism, the claim that former president Barack Obama is not a natural-born citizen.

Far from a fringe belief, birtherism—a movement led by Donald Trump—has remained popular among Republicans in the years since Obama left office. A 2017 YouGov poll found that 57 percent of Trump voters said it was "definitely true" or "probably true" that Obama is from Kenya.[7] In a Reddit thread on Obama's identity, a comment from a now-deleted account articulated birtherism in its purest form: "[Obama] isn't part of us, and therefore shouldn't rule us, and he has harmed us immensely and is our enemy. His race precludes him from legitimately ruling over us and his actions prove him evil and our enemy. Personally I think it seems likely he's a muslim in the islamic sense of the word. That is, that he said the shahada at some point of his life, likely Indonesia."

Former Republican senator Rick Santorum, a pro-Trump fixture on CNN, articulated the (only slightly) watered-down GOP version of birtherism, saying in 2010 that Obama was "detached from the American experience. He just doesn't identify with the average American because of his own background. Indonesia and Hawaii." Iowa Republican Steve King—who once said comparing immigrants to dogs was a compliment, and whose racist remarks eventually cost him his

House committee assignments—insisted that Obama's vision of America "isn't like our vision of America. That we know. Now I don't assert where he was born, I will just tell you that we are all certain that he was not raised with an American experience. So these things that beat in our hearts when we hear the National Anthem and when we say the Pledge of Allegiance doesn't beat the same for him."[8]

The demonization of Barack Obama as un-American, or *anti*-American, symbolizes the extremist view—now mainstreamed by the GOP—that Democrats and liberals are not merely inauthentic but dangerous to the republic. "Huge numbers of voters on the right believe that Democrats are not the loyal opposition, but are evil and intent on destroying America," tweeted William Dietz, a self-described "disgusted ex-Republican." Daryl Johnson, a former Department of Homeland Security analyst, told the *Washington Post*'s Greg Sargent that "the viciousness of the rhetoric painting Democrats as evil and corrupt" was a factor in the increase in right-wing extremist violence.[9] In the minds of many Republicans, Democrats have no standing to fight for America because it isn't theirs to fight for.

Bill Mitchell, a Donald Trump acolyte with more than four hundred thousand followers, tweeted, "The modern #DemocratParty is no less an enemy of America than #NaziGermany or #CommunistRussia was. They seek our complete and utter destruction as the greatest nation on earth." Mitchell's view is commonplace on right-wing media. The creator of a Facebook page titled "Democrats Hate America" complained that "every day, Democrats take the side of criminals, illegal aliens, and foreigners over law-abiding U.S. citizens." The graphic on the group's page depicts an enraged donkey holding a pistol to Uncle Sam's head.

When Democratic senator Jeff Merkley tweeted about Trump's friendliness with foreign dictators and asked his voters what they would tell their children about supporting him, Twitter user "Hardcore patriot" promptly fired back, "I'll tell my grandkids, your grandpa and father (along with millions of other patriots) helped the President save America from corruption, economic collapse and communism. Protecting our great constitution against liberal, America hating traitors." Journalist Wajahat Ali received a similar retort when he noted that Trump fans had lost the support of athletes, entertainers, and people of color. Trump supporter "America First" replied, "And we kept our dignity, love of country and flag and respect for military, vets and cops. The exit door is wide open Liberal Traitors. MAGA."

The right's depiction of Democrats as enemies and traitors draws on propaganda techniques used by authoritarian regimes. Yale philosopher Jason Stanley explained that in the rhetoric of extreme nationalists, "a glorious past has been lost by the humiliation brought on by globalism, liberal cosmopolitanism, and respect for 'universal values' such as equality. These values are supposed to have made the nation weak in the face of real and threatening challenges to the nation's existence." In *How Fascism Works: The Politics of Us and Them,* Stanley noted that these myths "are generally based on fantasies of a non-existent past uniformity, which survives in the traditions of the small towns and countrysides that remain relatively unpolluted by the liberal decadence of the cities."[10]

The concept of urban decadence is central to the "real American" narrative, drawing on the longstanding myth that big cities (predominantly Democratic) are dens of iniquity and small towns (predominantly Republican) bastions of rectitude. The rural-urban divide has a long history in American politics. "You can draw a straight line from the Jeffersonians in the late 18th century to the agrarian populists in the late 19th century to Mr. Trump's voters, all of whom have felt that the city hornswoggled the country," economic historian Louis Hyman wrote. He argued that there is a misguided nostalgia for a long-lost Main Street that embodies "a feeling of community and of having control over your life. It's everything, in short, that seems threatened by global capitalism and cosmopolitan elites in big cities and fancy suburbs."[11] Robert Wuthnow, author of *The Left Behind: Decline and Rage in Rural America,* wrote that "politically and religiously conservative people who live in small towns, on farms, and in sparsely populated areas far from either coast . . . consider their communities the heartland of America."[12]

The Washington establishment exploits rural-urban tensions, waxing rhapsodic about small towns to counter its elitist image. Right-wing proponents of the "real American" storyline go a step further by extolling the virtues of small towns to advance a whitewashed view of America, where city dwellers (code for people of color) are less American than their rural (code for white) counterparts. But economist Jed Kolko debunked the myth that the "real" America exists in some small, landlocked town. In his article "'Normal America' Is Not a Small Town of White People," Kolko argued that the notion "normal America is out there somewhere in a hamlet where they can't pronounce 'Acela' is misplaced." In fact, as Kolko explained, "it's not in a small town at all. I calculated how demographically similar each U.S. metropolitan area is to the U.S. overall, based on age, educational attainment, and race and ethnicity. The index equals 100 if a metro's demographic mix were identical to that of the U.S. overall. By this measure, the metropolitan area that looks most like the U.S. is New Haven, Connecticut, followed by Tampa, Florida, and Hartford, Connecticut."[13]

The idea of coastal hubs as less American is one of several fallacies about American identity and history uncritically woven into mainstream media coverage. One of those fallacies is that the working class is white and male. The term "white working class," wrote Alec MacGillis and ProPublica, has "served to conjure a vast swath of salt-of-the-earth citizens living and working in the wide-open spaces between the coasts—Sarah Palin's 'real America.'"[14] But as author Tamara Draut pointed out, "Far too often, the term 'working class' is conflated with white and male identities, frequently used as a short-hand to conjure the former archetype of the working class as a white man who works in manufacturing."[15]

Journalist Victoria A. Brownworth, a prominent member of the resistance and author of *Coming Out of Cancer: Writings from the Lesbian Cancer Epidemic*, tweeted, "We've been inculcated to believe the working class is white and male and it behooves white men to promote that narrative. The actual stats are directly opposite." In an article for DAME, Brownworth argued that "working class Americans evoke a consistent image: white men in hard hats and work boots who have fallen on hard economic times, the types of characters you'd find in a novel by John Steinbeck or Upton Sinclair. The problem is, this narrative of the working class is all wrong. It's not white men who hold the most jobs that fuel our economy; it's women, and disproportionately women of color at that."[16]

Author Nancy Isenberg emphasized to *Politico* that "the working class today has a large portion that are women, that are people of color. But when you look at the images at [Trump's] rallies—you know, people in their Bubba caps and their truckers' caps—that fits into a certain stereotype: poor white working-class men."[17] In her book *White Trash: The 400-Year Untold History of Class in America*, Isenberg traced the evolution of the "forgotten American"—a common refrain in mainstream coverage of the white working class. She described President Nixon's attempts "to appeal to a different breed of 'forgotten Americans' than those embraced by FDR's New Deal," noting that "those whom Nixon wished to connect with were the 'White Lower Middle

Class' . . . They were the alienated 'rabble,' and Nixon promised to embrace the 'Silent Majority' as the backbone of America—hardworking and true."[18]

The story of the "forgotten" white working-class voter is epitomized in a June 2016 exchange between *Morning Joe* host Joe Scarborough and former vice president Joe Biden, transcribed by the *Washington Post*:

SCARBOROUGH: We all are asking about Donald Trump. You're talking about a guy who's connecting with those workers in Scranton, Pennsylvania, who's connecting with those people in Youngstown, Ohio, who's connecting with those white, working-class voters in a way that you have your entire career—and a way that Hillary Clinton is not. You can just look at the numbers right now. Why is that?

BIDEN: That's why I'm going to be living in Pennsylvania and Ohio and Michigan—

SCARBOROUGH:—over the next six months. But why is that?

BIDEN: I think it's two reasons. One, I think the Democratic Party overall hasn't spoken enough to those voters. They've done the right thing for the voters—haven't spoken *to* them . . .

SCARBOROUGH: Have Democrats stopped talking to white, working-class voters?

BIDEN: I think we have, in part. And the reason is we've been consumed with crisis after crisis after crisis. And so I go in my old neighborhoods, and they go, "Joe. Hey, Joe, over here. What about me?"[19]

Biden and Scarborough make several assumptions in their conversation, among them that white working-class voters are neglected by Democrats, that there is a special way to connect to them, and that Trump and Biden have mastered it. But do the facts support those assumptions? No, says the *Washington Post*: "If being working class means being in the bottom half of the income distribution, the vast majority of Trump supporters during the primaries were not working class . . . the narrative that attributes Trump's victory to a 'coalition of mostly blue-collar white and working-class voters' just doesn't square with the 2016 election data."[20]

Scarborough's (oft-repeated) assertion that Hillary Clinton didn't appeal to the working class is also contradicted by the facts. Clinton won decisively among voters with annual incomes under $50,000. In an article titled "The Dangerous Myth That Hillary Clinton Ignored the Working Class," author and journalist Derek Thompson made the case that Hillary Clinton "talked about the working class, middle-class jobs, and the dignity of work constantly. And she still lost." Thompson noted that Clinton "detailed plans to help coal miners and steel workers . . . She talked about the dignity of manufacturing jobs, the promise of clean-energy jobs . . . She said the word 'job' more in the Democratic National Convention speech than Trump did in the RNC acceptance speech."[21] But despite the clear flaws in their 2016 narratives, America's leading media publications have doubled down on the "real American" story line, clinging to the idea that Trump's MAGA voters are misunderstood, under-covered, and unappreciated. Consider the subgenre of reporting that emerged in the immediate aftermath of the 2016 election, the circular *Trump supporters support Trump.*

"As Critics Assail Trump, His Supporters Dig in Deeper," blared the *New York Times*, following the outcry over the Trump administration's "zero tolerance" border policy. "For many Republicans," wrote the *Times*, "the audio of children sobbing at a migrant detention center barely registered, because these voters don't pay attention to the left-leaning and traditional media that have covered the family separation crisis far more than their preferred channel, Fox News."[22] A CNN story titled "What Trump Supporters Think of Family Separations at the Border" quoted a female Trump supporter at an Arizona diner scoffing at abused migrant children: "I think people need to stop constantly bringing up the poor children, the poor children. The parents are the problems. They're the ones coming in illegally. Quit trying to make us feel teary-eyed for the children." Another Trump voter compared caging children to the time he was fined for swimming in a lake: "These people that we have coming across the border illegally are breaking the rules. I have no feelings for them at all."[23]

After Trump's widely denounced Helsinki summit with Russian president Vladimir Putin—where his obsequiousness toward the Russian leader and attacks on the FBI led to accusations of treason—the *New York Times* rushed to get the perspective of Trump's diehard rust-belt fans. "At a bar in central Pennsylvania, voters wondered if election meddling was really so terrible," the *Times* reported.[24] Not to be outdone, *USA Today* followed with "President Trump's Voters Remain Loyal, Even as Mueller's Russia Investigation Intensifies." The story featured a Brownsburg, Indiana, plumber insisting that Trump's dealings with Russia were "just right."[25]

"Trump Voters Hit Hard by Tariffs Are Standing by Him—for Now," announced the *Washington Post.*[26] Reuters echoed the *Post*: "Iowa Farmers Wary of Aid, Trade Wars but Still Turn Out for Trump."[27] NBC ran a segment titled "Their Industries Are Hurting, but Voters Still Back Trump's Trade Policy."[28] NPR declared: "Voters in Florida's Panhandle Still Have Faith in Trump's Foreign Policy."[29]

By 2018, the genre had become so oversaturated that HuffPost ran a piece titled "Enough Already with the 'Trump Voters Still Like Trump' Stories."[30] On Twitter, attorney Kevin McNamee wrote that "the NY Times' great takeaway from its 2016 coverage was that its reporters were too tough on Trump voters. We've been inundated with 'Trump voters in

#RustBeltDiners' stories since." Comedian Andy Richter captured the genre's overkill in a pithy tweet: "'The forgotten American' has been interviewed 8,000 times."

After Democrats regained control of the House in the 2018 midterms, Oliver Willis, an inveterate media watcher, prodded mainstream reporters: "Where are our heartland diner stories? Our profiles of surging voters who 'upset the status quo' with 'maverick politicians'? How come voters in blue states that got bluer and purple states that went blue and red districts that flipped aren't getting the Trump voter treatment? It would make one think that gosh, this whole thing about the media being liberal is bullshit, and that the mainstream media caters to Republican whims while minimizing the rest of us no matter the political power we display. Imagine!"[31]

Eric Boehlert, author of *Lapdogs: How the Press Rolled Over for Bush*, criticized the *New York Times* for failing to cover right-wing extremism among Trump supporters. Referring to the October 2018 mail bomber, Boehlert tweeted, "Funny how NYT has published what, 350 Trump voter puff pieces . . . yet *never* acknowledged people like this. NYT was *certain* the Trump base was made up only of (white) hard working, forgotten Americans." Boehlert knocked the *Times* again when it ran a piece about suburban men backing Trump ("He's tough, he's a bully, but boy things are getting done," said an Ohio businessman[32]). Boehlert responded: "GUYS, the Times went to a GOP district in a red state to interview white Trump supporters . . . if you were [a] reporter in Oct 2010 and pitched

[the] idea of going to Baltimore to interview black voters abt why they supported Obama, you would've been laughed out of every newsroom."

Imani Gandy, senior legal analyst at Rewire.News, tweeted mockingly, "BREAKING NEWS FROM THE NEW YORK TIMES: White women who voted for trump really like trump; think he's a swell guy; and is actually quite groovy." *Rolling Stone* writer Jamil Smith quote-tweeted a *Times* article titled "Across South, Democrats Risk Speaking Boldly and Alienating Rural White Voters." Flipping the headline, Smith tweeted, "I'm looking forward to the sequel to this article, 'Across America, Republicans Risk Speaking Boldly and Alienating Voters of Color.'" Nai Mei Yao, a doctor and activist, challenged the *Times*: "It really would be nice if the NY Times, as a change of pace, went around the country and highlighted EACH policy Trump has affected since getting into office and found people HURT by these policies and explained WHY."

Undeterred by the criticism, the @NYTPolitics account tweeted a public call to its followers: "Are you a person of color who has been criticized by others in your community for being a conservative or supporting Donald Trump? We want to hear from you." The tweet sparked a furious response. Twitter user Erin Leahy shot back, "How about instead of profiling Trump supporters—whether they are black, white, slightly orange, or purple, you ask the marginalized communities who are being denied the right to vote in this election? Just once. Just this one time." Freelance editor and writer Veronica Marie poked fun at the paper, tweeting, "I can't wait for the next pitch: 'Are you a Trump-supporting dog or cat with a Democratic owner? Do you feel oppressed or discriminated against for your preferences? Are they restricting your access to toys & premium kibble because of it? We want to hear from you!'"

The subtext of the mainstream media's inordinate focus on MAGA voters is that the opinions and grievances of "real Americans"—white working-class small-town Republicans—take precedence over those of other voters, particularly the voters of color who make up the Democratic base. Newsrooms have sought out Americans whose support for nativist GOP policies is said to be motivated by "economic anxiety." Investigative reporter Nikole Hannah-Jones rejected that approach, arguing that "these claims about white people voting for Trump based on economic anxiety and not race never stood up to scrutiny because 1) Typical Trump supporter wasnt working-class 2) This logic could never explain why economically anxious folks from other racial groups ALL went HRC." "Propane Jane," a Texas-based doctor and digital activist, tweeted bluntly, "When fascism came to America it was wrapped in the Confederate flag and renamed 'economic anxiety' by the MSM."

Political strategist Adam Jentleson argued that "too often it seems like the newsroom conversation is about how to bend over backwards to avoid using accurate language. That's how we end up being fed terms like 'racially charged' and 'provocateur.'" NPR host Sam Sanders admonished reporters, "Don't say 'suburban voters' when you mean 'white suburban voters.' Don't say evangelical voters when you mean 'white evangelical voters.' Don't say 'working class voters' when you mean 'white working class voters.' It's best when journalists deal in specifics, not avoidance."

During the 2016 election, Donald Trump's explicitly racist comments and open embrace of white nationalism found an enthusiastic audience on the right, but it was well into his presidency before the media establishment openly acknowledged the role race played in his campaign. As Vox reported a year after the election, "There have now been numerous studies that found support for Trump is closely linked to racial resentment, defined by [researchers] Fowler, Medenica, and Cohen as 'a moral feeling that blacks violate such traditional American values as individualism and self-reliance.'"[33] The *New York Times* pointed out that in 2016, "White, Christian and male, voters . . . turned to Mr. Trump because they felt their status was at risk."[34] This was also Trump's 2018 midterm strategy, political commentator Mike Barnicle noted. "The basic appeal, to put it on the table, is whiteness. That is what the president seems to be doing," Barnicle said.[35]

As journalist Sabrina Tavernise explained, for white nationalists, "the moment when white Americans will make up less than half the country's population . . . signifies a kind of doomsday clock counting down to the end of racial and cultural dominance."[36] The Republican Party has responded to these demographic changes by veering to the far right. Michael

Harriot, columnist at The Root, wrote that the GOP "is now the party of the alt-right. It is the party of the Willie Horton ad and birtherism. It is the party of Donald Trump, the 'Muslim ban,' the border wall, David Duke and all the other white suprem-acists running for election on the Republican ticket." Harriot continued, "And none of this is to say that all Republicans are racist. There is a legitimate debate to be had about economic conservatism, small government and trickle-down economics (Well . . . Maybe not trickle-down economics), but the GOP has doubled down on racism."[37]

Chicago Tribune columnist Dahleen Glanton addressed the claim that Trump supporters are maligned and misunder-stood—that they are unfairly painted with a broad brush of racism. "After I recently wrote a column lamenting what drives Trump's 40 percent base, the president's supporters bombarded me with emails," Glanton wrote. "Not all Trump supporters, they insist, get their views from Fox News' Sean Hannity, but rather they are hardworking, informed Americans who believe the economic advantages of having Trump in office outweigh any social disadvantages." Glanton offered a counterpoint: "Yes, Trump does have an agenda for immigration. It's to keep nonwhites and non-Christians from entering this country. And what about those tariffs? How are they working out for the working class?"

Glanton rejected the idea that white Americans are unduly burdened: "Trump supporters aren't the only group in America who are disillusioned and worried about their futures. Ask

African-Americans, Latinos, Muslims, gay people, transgender people and impoverished Americans how hopeful they feel under Trump's leadership."[38] If anything, as historian Joshua Zeitz argued, whiteness "continues to pay tangible benefits . . . It makes one less likely to be killed by a police officer during a traffic stop. It enables white men to carry assault weapons (including long guns) in places of public accommodation, while a black man might be shot and killed by law enforcement officials merely for picking up a BB gun displayed on a sales rack at Walmart. It affords working-class white families the peace of mind that the government won't invade homes or hospitals in pursuit of undocumented children or grandparents."[39]

But a Twitter user named "Why?" disputed the idea of white privilege: "I'm sick of #SJW [social justice warrior] types saying that as an heterosexual white male I'm in a position of power backed up by western patriarchy. I can honestly say I've never felt in a position of power in my entire life! So fuck off!!" Clinical psychologist Jordan B Peterson, a popular right-wing internet personality, argued that "the idea of white privilege is absolutely reprehensible."[40] On Reddit, "wazzup987" argued that "what we have is the vast majority of whites being like I'm not rich, I'm not privileged, all they see is jobs going away and their communities getting poorer and more desperate with drug use on the rise while some social justice twit with a worthless degree tells them how privileged[tm] they are for white skin and a penis and how all the ills of the world are because of their race." This message of white grievance permeates right-wing media. CNN's Brian Stelter noted that "on Fox's highest-rated shows, the politics of white anxiety play out practically every day, as hosts and guests warn about the impacts of immigration and minimize or mock the perspectives of POC."

In her bestselling book *White Rage: The Unspoken Truth of Our Racial Divide,* Emory University professor Carol Anderson wrote that the trigger for white rage—variously referred to in the media as white anxiety, white grievance, or white resentment—is "black advancement." As Anderson explained, "It is not the mere presence of black people that is the problem; rather, it is blackness with ambition, with drive, with purpose, with aspirations, and with demands for full and equal citizenship. It is blackness that refuses to accept subjugation, to give up. And all the while, white rage manages to maintain not only the upper hand, but also, apparently, the moral high ground."[41]

Anderson's point that white rage maintains "the moral high ground" is worth highlighting. Democrats, progressives, and principled conservatives often assume that their criticisms of the GOP's extremist policies are self-evidently true, but MAGA Republicans are indignant and defiant about *their* moral arguments. "Isn't that nice of Mr Obama? Good for his virtue signaling!" tweeted CNN political commentator Jack Kingston about Barack Obama volunteering at a food bank on Thanksgiving. "Now thx to #Trump 4million less people are on food stamps, there are more jobs than workers, African American, Hispanic & female unemployment levels are at historic lows. It's pretty obvious who has helped the poor most!" Kingston asserted.

What Democrats assail as the GOP's dehumanization and abuse of migrants, the right spins as a defense of American sovereignty against invading "illegals." Support for a woman's reproductive freedom is characterized by the right as a desire to murder babies. The progressive push for universal health care is portrayed by the right as a pernicious form of government intrusion. Desperate calls for sensible measures to protect schoolchildren from gun violence are rejected by the right as a subversion of the Second Amendment. And attempts to confront systemic racism are met with right-wing claims that white working-class Republicans are *themselves* the besieged and aggrieved party, selflessly defending American values from the profligacy of liberals, people of color, immigrants, and Muslims.

NPR's Don Gonyea reported that a majority of white Americans believe they are discriminated against. Gonyea quoted an Ohio man complaining, "If you apply for a job, they seem to give the blacks the first crack at it, and basically, you know, if you want any help from the government, if you're white, you don't get it. If you're black, you get it."[42] Political theorist Juliet Hooker provided historical context for this siege mentality. In her book *Race and the Politics of Solidarity*, Hooker explained, "To the extent that most whites in the United States believe that racism was a temporary aberration from a norm of racial justice that has since been corrected, for example, they tend to view remedies for racialized oppression today as 'special,' unwarranted rights for African Americans."[43]

More than a century and a half after the Civil War, the structural racism coded into America's DNA remains the great dividing line in the red-blue fight. "The Founding Fathers built white dominance into the fabric and laws of the nation, and a country that proclaims to love freedom and liberty is still struggling with its roots in the original sin of slavery," wrote journalist Michele Norris.[44] Filmmaker and resistance favorite Rob Reiner struck a note of optimism, predicting that the GOP "will lose this last big battle of the Civil War. Diversity is our strength."

TWO

BATTLE FOR TRUTH: ENEMIES OF THE PEOPLE

The truth knocks on the door and you say, "Go away, I'm
looking for the truth," and so it goes away. Puzzling.
—Robert Pirsig, *Zen and the Art of*
Motorcycle Maintenance

The durability of the "real American" story—the fiction that small-town white Christian Republicans are the authentic Americans, and that they are besieged by liberals, elites, and brown invaders—relies on effective storytellers, receptive listeners, and the "willing suspension of disbelief," a term coined by Samuel Taylor Coleridge to explain how readers might believe "shadows of imagination." The trick, Coleridge wrote, was to infuse a tale with "a human interest and a semblance of truth."[1]

Right-wing media have adopted Coleridge's prescription, building an integrated messaging system that manipulates public opinion by focusing on a human interest story (e.g., a crime by an undocumented immigrant); setting up a straw-man argument (Democrats want to let dangerous "illegals" into the country); dressing it up in the "real American" frame ("true patriots" of the heartland are fighting back); and shielding it from scrutiny by attacking other, more credible news sources. This strategy, honed over decades, has molded the views of a generation of Republican voters, who perceive far-right propaganda as truth and verifiable facts as deceptions.

"On the right, millions of people wake up with 'Fox & Friends,' commute with talk radio, have lunch with Limbaugh, or settle in for an evening of Carlson, Hannity and Ingraham, as their president tweets against the fake news media," Harvard Law School professor Yochai Benkler told the *Washington Post*.[2] This right-wing echo chamber reinforces itself by dismissing credible news sources as "fake news" and "liberal media." The effect is to degrade trust in the fourth estate, corrode faith in facts and truth, and undermine opposing ideological perspectives.

"Long before Fox News, before [Roger] Ailes and Rush Limbaugh and Sean Hannity, there was a conservative media complex in the United States refining a theory of liberal media bias," wrote *Messengers of the Right* author Nicole Hemmer.[3] Conservatives, she said, "viewed objectivity as a mask concealing entrenched liberal bias, hiding the slanted reporting that dominated American media." In a *Washington Post* op-ed titled "How Republicans Trick Facebook and Twitter with Claims of Bias," author and professor Nikki Usher explained that "playing the ref" as a political tactic "dates back at least to

Barry Goldwater's presidential campaign, in which Goldwater handed out 'Eastern liberal press' pins to journalists." Usher noted that "it reached fever pitch during the paranoid years of the Nixon administration, saw great success in Reagan-era arguments against the fairness doctrine and has remained critical to the GOP playbook in the decades since."[4]

Liberal media bias is one of the most ingrained beliefs in American politics, treated as gospel by Republicans and uncritically accepted by nearly a quarter of Democrats. An August 2018 Ipsos poll found that 80 percent of Republicans and 23 percent of Democrats agreed that "most news outlets have a liberal bias."[5] It is such an article of faith on the right "that to deny it is to deny that the sun came up in the morning," wrote Heather "Digby" Parton, a popular progressive blogger. Parton argued that the belief is predicated on "ignoring the fact that most media companies are owned or run by wealthy conservatives."[6] As Parton suggests, proponents of the "liberal media" myth focus on the political leanings of individual journalists, ignoring the corporate incentives that drive editorial decisions. But mainstream media companies are businesses and their natural bias is toward balance sheets and bottom lines.

In 2016, CBS chairman Les Moonves raised eyebrows when he said, "Donald's place in this election is a good thing . . . The money's rolling in and this is fun." Moonves—who later resigned after several women accused him of sexual misconduct—admitted, "It may not be good for America, but it's damn good for CBS."[7] When cable networks came under fire for airing live Trump speeches peppered with lies and mis-statements, journalist and anchor Soledad O'Brien was skeptical that the practice would stop, tweeting, "The financial model depends on this."

Corporate media ownership was the subject of a column by journalist James Warren titled "Consolidation Is Killing the Myth of the Liberal Media." Warren wrote, "The power of caricature is potent and it includes the press as privacy invading, circulation grabbing liberals. That's always been dubious, especially if you look at corporate ownership. Now, you've got not just unceasing consolidation but the unceasing influence of folks of distinctly conservative ideology."[8] Indeed, the "liberal media" attack has provided cover for right-wing media companies to advance their mission and grow their audience. "Fox News is just the tip of the iceberg," explained media studies professor Chuck Tryon, noting that Sinclair Broadcast Group "has bought up hundreds of network affiliates across the country and requires them to carry 'must-run' segments during local news broadcasts that push a conservative agenda."[9]

The right-wing media ecosystem, which includes Fox News, Sinclair, talk radio, Drudge, and partisan websites and social media pages, maximizes its impact by positioning itself as a counterpoint to an allegedly dishonest and unpatriotic left-leaning national press—Trump's "enemies of the people." And Republicans eat it up. A July 2018 CBS News poll found that 91 percent of Trump supporters trusted him for "accurate information," 63 percent trusted "friends and family," and only

11 percent trusted the mainstream media.[10] Fifty-one percent of Republican voters in an August 2018 Quinnipiac University poll viewed the news media as an "enemy of the people."[11] For perspective, *The Hill* reported that trust in media "was once at 74 percent in 1976 in the post-Watergate reporting era."[12]

Trump's inauguration consummated the marriage between the GOP and right-wing media. In the first two years of his presidency, Trump repeatedly expressed views lifted from Fox News segments. At a November 2018 rally in Rush Limbaugh's hometown of Cape Girardeau, Missouri, Trump was joined onstage by Fox News hosts Sean Hannity and Jeanine Pirro. Limbaugh was in attendance. Weeks later, the *Hollywood Reporter* revealed that, as part of a severance package, White House communications chief and former Fox News executive Bill Shine would be "paid simultaneously by both the White House and the parent company of Fox News."[13] The key players in the right-wing media apparatus were now at the pinnacle of U.S. politics, prompting political science professor Thomas Schaller to tweet, "It's not hyperbole to say that the combination of Limbaugh Hannity Coulter and Ingraham have more influence over Trump than any appointed or elected officials."

Trump—whose mastery of Fox-style narratives goes a long way to account for his rise to the presidency—laid bare his media strategy to *60 Minutes* correspondent Lesley Stahl: "You know why I [attack the press]? I do it to discredit you all and demean you all so when you write negative stories about me, no one will believe you. So, put that in your head for a minute."[14] By discrediting the press, Trump "discredits criticism and scrutiny of his administration, character and words," wrote *USA Today* opinion contributor Dick Meyer. "He discredits the idea that truth and facts exist."[15] This assault on truth is a deliberate strategy, explained Yale University historian Timothy Snyder. "A basic weapon of regime changers," Snyder wrote, "is to destroy the concept of truth. Democracy requires the rule of law, the rule of law depends upon trust, and trust depends upon citizens' acceptance of factuality. The president and his aides actively seek to destroy Americans' sense of reality." Snyder's conclusion: "Post-factuality is pre-fascism."[16]

Rational discourse is anathema to extremists. Under the influence of the far right, Republican officials have worked relentlessly to degrade America's shared sense of truth and reality. "What you are seeing and what you are reading is not what is happening," Trump declared. "Truth isn't truth," Trump's personal attorney Rudy Giuliani told NBC's Chuck Todd. "Facts are in the eye of the beholder," he said to CNN's Chris Cuomo. Former White House press secretary Sean Spicer's false statements were "alternative facts," asserted senior White House adviser Kellyanne Conway. And Trump attorney Jay Sekulow told ABC's George Stephanopoulos that "over time, facts develop."

Daniel Dale, Washington bureau chief of the *Toronto Star*, amassed more than half a million Twitter followers by chronicling Trump's daily torrent of false claims and lies. One glaring example was Trump's assertion that only 3 percent of people released for an asylum hearing appeared in court. The truth, Dale tweeted, is that "his Justice Department says it was 89% [in 2017], 91% in 2016, 93% in 2015, 94% in 2014." These flagrant attacks on veracity and accuracy are rhetorical sledgehammers aimed at the foundations of civil discourse, calculated to protect a far-right worldview by undercutting contrary reality-based perspectives.

In early November 2018, *Washington Post* reporter Matt Viser quoted Trump saying, "I'm the only one who ever tells you the facts." In response, author Cameron Conaway tweeted, "Trump's goal (thanks in part to ideas Bannon planted) has been to discredit all major media outlets + stoke a variety of mini civil wars so he can consolidate power by positioning himself as the single source of truth." Leah McElrath, a prominent resistance activist, quote-tweeted Viser with a truncated passage from Hannah Arendt's *The Origins of Totalitarianism*: "The ideal subject of totalitarian rule is not the convinced Nazi or the convinced Communist, but people for whom the distinction between fact and fiction" and "the distinction between true and false no longer exist." Simply put, "the 'truth' is broken," said author and activist Amy Siskind. Even Guns N' Roses singer Axl Rose joined the chorus, tweeting that Trump "says what's real is fake n' what's fake is real."

The Republican Party's war on truth is part of a multi-pronged strategy that includes attacks on the mainstream press and harassment of progressive activists on digital media platforms. *Bloomberg* columnist Noah Smith wrote that "online harassment is pervasive, and that social media is the main vector for those attacks."[17] Pollster Celinda Lake tweeted that "female journalists and politicians receive abuse on @twitter every 30 seconds. Women of color are 34% more likely to be targeted than white women; black women are 84% more likely to receive abuse than white women."

Independent human rights and democracy watchdog Freedom House warned against "digital authoritarianism," arguing that for democracy to thrive citizens must have "access to a public forum that allows rational discourse."[18] But rational discourse is in short supply in American politics, due in no small part to social media's acrimony, the traditional media's loss of credibility, and right-wing media's reality distortion field. (*Rolling Stone*'s Tim Dickinson once described Fox News as "a giant soundstage created to mimic the look and feel of a news operation, cleverly camouflaging political propaganda as independent journalism."[19])

As the "liberal media" myth has evolved into a coordinated GOP offensive against the free press, mainstream reporters have struck back. CNN's Jim Acosta, a frequent right-wing target, tweeted, "Imagine what life would be like if the only 'trusted' news source is the government, mandating what's reported and controlling what appears in internet search engine results. I've visited places like that. They are not the United States of America." Less than three months after that tweet, the Secret Service denied Acosta entrance to the White House. His press pass had been revoked after a testy exchange with Trump at a post-midterm press conference. CNN called the administration's behavior "a stunning break with protocol"[20] and successfully sued to reinstate Acosta's pass. White House correspondent April Ryan—another target of right-wing rage—spoke at Yale University about the challenges and risks of reporting during such a fraught time: "When they say we can't ask a question or that we're fake, it's about you, because without us you don't get the information. It's been made to be about us, which is sad because now we are getting death threats . . . It's now deadly to do the job."[21]

Despite occasional counterpunching by responsible journalists, the relentless "liberal media" mantra has had the desired effect. Reporters reflexively overcorrect to avoid the dreaded liberal bias tag, and far-right narratives regularly seep into mainstream coverage. Progressive activists have criticized the establishment media for coddling the Trump administration. Reporters, including Jonathan Swan of Axios and Maggie Haberman of the *New York Times*, have come under sustained criticism for "access journalism"—and the critiques are not just from the political left. Bruce Bartlett, who served as a domestic policy adviser to Ronald Reagan, tweeted, "The NYT continuously debases itself pandering to right-wingers so they won't criticize it for being left-wing. Utterly stupid. Gains no right-wing readers, loses liberal readers who are disgusted." Political columnist Lauren Duca argued that journalism "is not about striving to appear fair, but maintaining a rigorous objectivity for the purpose of serving the public." She concluded that, on the whole, "journalists are routinely failing to uphold and communicate their utmost duty: to empower citizens with the information needed to hold those in power accountable."[22]

Facing coordinated attacks from the right and fierce criticism from Democrats that they are caving to the pressure, the mainstream media take solace in an illusion of balance. But Andrew Stroehlein, European Media Director of Human Rights Watch, was blunt about the danger of false equivalence: "'Well, we get criticized both by people calling for mass murder and by people opposed to mass murder, so we must be getting things about right.'—essentially how many mainstream media outlets are justifying their absurd definition of 'balance' today." Zerlina Maxwell, a prominent progressive political analyst, tweeted, "I mean there will be literal nazis marching in the streets before the msm realizes that calling for civility from both sides is stupid. Wait. Too late." The *New Yorker*'s Adam Davidson argued that "both-sidism operates at every level . . . It is shoved into the brains of newbies and a source of enormous pride for veterans." Television critic James Poniewozik chimed in, tweeting, "I'm just gonna be a crank for a minute. The job of journalism is not to appear unbiased. The job of journalism is to accurately describe the world as you find it. If you think the first thing is more important than the second, you picked the wrong job."

As the culture war has migrated online, the "liberal bias" strategy has moved with it. On the right, "Social Media Bias Is the New Liberal Media Bias," wrote Elliot Hannon for

Slate, who pointed out that the new right-wing enemy "isn't necessarily the New York Times, but Google, Facebook, and Twitter."[23] According to Axios, "65% of self-described conservatives believe that social media companies purposely censor the right."[24] The Daily Beast reported that "pro-Trump Twitter users are increasingly registering their discontent with [Twitter CEO Jack] Dorsey by adding a red 'X' emoji to their account names to claim they're being 'shadow-banned.'"[25]

The hashtag #StopTheBias has been used by prominent Republicans, including House minority leader Kevin McCarthy, to highlight what they claim is liberal bias in the tech world. "Another day, another example of conservatives being censored on social media," McCarthy wrote, after his quote-tweet of Fox News host Laura Ingraham was flagged for sensitive content. But the snafu was caused by McCarthy's personal account settings, not liberal tech bias. Historian and professor Kevin M. Kruse tweeted at McCarthy, "That's not Twitter censoring [Ingraham's] tweets. It's Twitter following your own personal account settings. My God, this is just embarrassing."

Replicating their "liberal media" strategy, Republicans have used accusations of social media bias to energize their online base and to build dedicated right-wing digital platforms. The *New York Times* reported that "far-right internet communities have been buoyed as their once-fringe views have been given oxygen by prominent Republicans."[26] *Politico* revealed that the Trump White House's communications office distributed talking points under the header "Big Tech is Suppressing

Conservative Voices."[27] Libertarian tech entrepreneur Declan McCullagh argued that "social media execs did themselves no favors by becoming so closely identified with the Democratic Party and, more broadly, the elite progressive left. Now the industry's politically charmed existence, in which it enjoyed deregulatory Republicans as allies, has come to an abrupt end."[28]

But the "liberal social media" claim, like its "liberal media" precursor, fails to hold up to serious examination. If anything, social media platforms have proven to be exceptionally favorable terrain for right-wing extremists. Tech reporter Maya Kosoff wrote that Facebook's platform design "has made it an incredibly effective tool for spreading explosive, viral right-wing messaging."[29] The Oxford Internet Institute found that on Facebook "extreme hard right pages—distinct from Republican pages—share the widest range of known junk news sources and circulate more junk news than all the other audiences put together."[30] The *New York Times* cited a landmark study of anti-refugee attacks in Germany that provided convincing evidence for "a phenomenon long suspected by researchers who study Facebook: that the platform makes communities more prone to racial violence."[31]

Casey Newton, Silicon Valley editor at The Verge, looked at hate speech on Facebook-owned Instagram. "More than ever before," he wrote, "journalists are finding vast swaths of hate speech on Instagram."[32] Tech writer Will Sommer wrote that "Instagram has become a surprising refuge for far-right figures who have somehow managed to avoid being banned from that site as well."[33] Right-wing extremists have also made effective use of YouTube. The *Guardian* reported that "YouTube provides a breeding ground for far-right radicalization, where people interested in conservative and libertarian ideas are quickly exposed to white nationalist ones."[34] According to reporter Kelly Weill, "YouTubers have learned to leverage the site's algorithms, frontloading their videos with terms like 'liberal' and 'intersectional' in a bid to 'hijack' search results that would typically be dominated by the left."[35]

Beyond the major social media sites, the far right uses encrypted messaging apps, social platforms, and internet forums such as Discord, 4chan, Gab, and Telegram to mobilize and communicate. A 2015 blog post by a former 4chan user traced the forum's influx of right-wing extremists: "There probably was never a moment were racism couldn't be found on 4chan, but the trend of making racist posts shifted drastically from being an ironic, edgy joke to a very serious habit for a percentage of the posters."[36]

Vice's Ben Makuch and Mack Lamoureux reported on a new digital platform designed to organize neo-Nazis, writing that "a neo-Nazi who goes by the alias Norman Spear has launched a project to unify online fascists and link that vast coalition of individuals into a network training new soldiers for a so-called forthcoming 'race war.'" According to Makuch and Lamoureux, Spear is "bringing neo-Nazis together, regardless of affiliation and ideology, into a militant fascist umbrella organization. His tool for doing this? A social network he calls 'The

Base,' which is already organizing across the US and abroad, specifically geared toward partaking in terrorism."[37]

Other technologies ripe for extremist exploitation include online games and "deepfakes," which the *New York Times* described as "an ultrarealistic fake video made with artificial intelligence software." As the *Times* reported, "Lawmakers have already begun to worry about how deepfakes could be used for political sabotage and propaganda."[38] Writing for *Foreign Affairs*, Robert Chesney and Danielle Citron predicted that "as deepfake technology develops and spreads, the current disinformation wars may soon look like the propaganda equivalent of the era of swords and shields."[39] Anya Kamenetz, NPR's lead education blogger, wrote that "while it's by no means common, online games, and the associated chat rooms, livestreams and other channels, have become one avenue for recruitment by right-wing extremist groups."[40]

The far right's use of social media to foment unrest was the subject of a NowThis video by digital strategist Melissa Ryan that racked up more than one million views. In it, Ryan explained that a coalition including "right-wing media, far-right online communities, home-grown hate groups, and hostile foreign actors, most notably Russian trolls," was using social platforms to exploit "our cultural and political weaknesses." Ryan highlighted four areas of social media weaponization: "false amplification, spreading disinformation, online harassment, and fanning the flames."[41]

Vanity Fair writer Mike Mariani compared the information landscape in the United States to the "sophisticated postmodern propaganda model developed by none other than Vladimir Putin, Vladislav Surkov, and their political technologists at the Kremlin." Elaborating on their Machiavellian tactics, Mariani explained that "what looked like a vibrant coalition of support for Russia's annexation [of Crimea] was really just the booming sound and fury of Kremlin *dramaturgia*." He added that Moscow "was choreographing the entire thing, directing its patriotic ensemble in order to confuse and misdirect the countries and international organizations that might otherwise have intervened against an act of war. At home, the effect was to warp Russians' sense of reality by clouding their vision and rousing their nationalism."[42]

Warping reality, clouding people's vision, and rousing nationalism: each is a pillar of far-right propaganda, and each is used by the GOP and right-wing media to stoke xenophobic impulses in the American electorate. Republican voters are consistently told that they are under attack by hordes of brown invaders. Crimes by undocumented immigrants are given priority coverage on Fox News and right-wing social media channels. During the early 2019 government shutdown over Trump's demands for a border wall, the Daily Beast's Olivia Messer reported that *Fox and Friends* cohost Ainsley Earhardt "spent the morning fear-mongering with context-free examples of violent crimes allegedly committed by undocumented immigrants in the United States, claiming that 'illegal aliens,' once in the country, will commit atrocities against American citizens and their families.'[43]

This nativist fearmongering was on ugly display in the summer of 2018, when University of Iowa student Mollie Tibbetts vanished after going for a jog in her Brooklyn, Iowa, neighborhood. She was found several weeks later, after Cristhian Rivera, an undocumented immigrant, confessed to killing her and guided investigators to her body. Rivera's crime was despicable, and tragically all too common. The Violence Policy Center's annual study *When Men Murder Women* found that more than 1,800 women were murdered by men in 2016, the most recent year for which data was available.[44]

Tibbetts's murder was immediately politicized by Republican lawmakers, who laced their condolences to the family with language about immigration policy. CNN reported that Republican governor Kim Reynolds "complained about a broken immigration system that allowed a 'predator' to live in her state," and that GOP senators Joni Ernst and Chuck Grassley "also sent condolences and called for action on illegal immigration."[45] Republican senator Tom Cotton tweeted, "Prayers for Tibbetts family & all who knew & loved Mollie. Lots of questions—where did this illegal alien work? what was his work status—but one thing is sure: Mollie would be alive if our government had taken immigration enforcement seriously years ago."

Mike Pence tweeted, "Heartbroken by the news about

Mollie Tibbetts. Mollie was an amazing young woman and we are praying for her parents, brothers & friends in this time of unimaginable grief . . . We commend the swift action by local, state, & federal investigators working in Iowa in apprehending an illegal immigrant, who's now charged with first-degree murder. Now, justice will be served. We will never forget Mollie Tibbetts." Campaigning at a West Virginia rally, Donald Trump said, "You heard about today with the illegal alien coming in very sadly from Mexico. And you saw what happened to that incredible beautiful young woman. Should have never happened."

The day after Tibbetts's body was discovered, "the killing was the lead item on nearly every prominent conservative website," journalist Eve Peyser reported.[46] And virtually all the headlines began with the word "illegal:"

Breitbart News: "Illegal Alien Charged with First Degree Murder of Mollie Tibbetts."[47]

Daily Caller: "Illegal Immigrant Charged with Murder of Iowa College Student Mollie Tibbetts."[48]

The Blaze: "Illegal immigrant charged with first-degree murder in Mollie Tibbetts' death."[49]

BuzzFeed News reported that on Facebook "an image that included Tibbetts's face encouraged voters to 'remember all the murdered Americans, and the illegal aliens that the Democrats care about more than they want to protect you.' The image was posted by multiple high-profile accounts and shared more than 100,000 times."[50] Media Matters, a nonprofit media watchdog, tracked the spike in Tibbetts coverage on Fox News, noting that it tripled "after law enforcement announced that the suspect was undocumented."[51] Axios reported that "Republicans Want to Make Mollie Tibbetts a Household Name,"[52] quoting former House Speaker Newt Gingrich crassly admitting to using her death as a midterm election strategy.

The mainstream press—taking its cue from right-wing media—amplified the Tibbetts story. *Paste*'s Shane Ryan argued that "the right has turned the [*New York Times*], along with many others, into an effective signal booster—the mainstream media serves as advocate and hype man, delivering an extremist message with almost total credulity to a far larger audience than the extremists could ever muster on their own." As Ryan noted, "Demonizing a specific racial group has a long and storied history on planet Earth, and has been a key tactic for fascist movements the world over. What's disheartening is how easily the American right has commandeered the narrative and essentially forced national media outlets like the *Times* and *Post* to cover these stories in a straight news fashion."[53]

Sensing the impending rush of media coverage, columnist Michael Tomasky tweeted, "Think about being that girl's parents and loved ones as Fox spends the next two days using her as a deflector shield." Tomasky didn't have to wonder what Mollie

Tibbetts's family was thinking. Her father, Rob Tibbetts, wrote a guest column for the *Des Moines Register* rebuking Republican politicians who had exploited her murder: "I encourage the debate on immigration; there is great merit in its reasonable outcome. But do not appropriate Mollie's soul in advancing views she believed were profoundly racist." Displaying the kind of magnanimity absent among GOP leaders taking advantage of his daughter's death, Rob Tibbetts wrote, "To the Hispanic community, my family stands with you and offers its heartfelt apology. That you've been beset by the circumstances of Mollie's death is wrong. We treasure the contribution you bring to the American tapestry in all its color and melody."[54]

The right's exploitation of Mollie Tibbetts's murder—over her family's objections—was widely criticized by Democrats and progressives. Political strategist Symone Sanders placed the Tibbetts killing in the context of the epidemic of male violence against women: "Mollie Tibbetts was murdered b/c she told a man to leave her alone while she was jogging. Her murderer happens to be undocumented. This isn't about border security. This is about toxic masculinity. Mollie Tibbetts lost her life b/c a man couldn't take her saying no. Full stop." As feminist author Jessica Valenti pointed out, "The deadliest demographic for American women isn't immigrants—it's husbands & boyfriends. But the truth about who kills women in this country isn't politically useful for the White House."

Attorney and organizer Alida Garcia admonished the press, "Dear Media: You can both be saddened & hurt by the tragedy of Mollie Tibbetts' killing, call for her perpetrator to be brought to swift justice, AND opt out of using a tragedy to criminalize all immigrants as guilty." Even Fox News correspondent Geraldo Rivera cried foul, telling host Martha MacCallum, "I know that most of the Fox audience disagrees with me, but I'm begging you to have compassion and not brand this entire population by the deeds of this one person." Unsurprisingly, right-wing media rejected the criticism that they were exploiting Tibbetts's murder, arguing that her death was preventable because her killer was not lawfully in the U.S., and that the story was thus legitimate political fodder. But on closer analysis, the right's argument falls apart.

First, the hyperfocus on crimes by undocumented immigrants implies immigrants are responsible for an inordinate amount of crime. But the data shows no correlation between increases in immigration and increases in crime. In fact, according to a Cato Institute study, "The vast majority of research finds that immigrants do not increase local crime rates and that they are less likely to cause crime and less likely to be incarcerated than their native-born peers."[55] A study published in the journal *Criminology* found that "undocumented immigration does not increase violence."[56]

Second, as right-wing media and GOP lawmakers clamored to politicize Tibbetts's murder, they were silent on other horrific killings that occurred during the same period:

Makiyah Wilson, 10, shot to death as she went to buy ice cream.

Kayden Mancuso, 7, killed by her biological father, Jeffrey Mancuso, a white male, after a lengthy custody battle with her mother.

Nia Wilson, 18, stabbed to death by a white male on a Bay Area Rapid Transit station platform in Oakland, California.

Casey Nicole Kizer, 17, killed near a Home Depot in Sylacauga, Alabama.

Shanann Watts (pregnant), 34, and her daughters Bella, 4, and Celeste, 3, murdered and buried by the husband and father, Chris Watts, a white male.

Not *one* of these victims was the subject of presidential speeches and tweets. Not one of the families was told "we will never forget" by the Vice President of the United States. Not one was treated as a Republican Party priority. Not one had thousands of MAGA accounts tweeting and posting about them months after the crime. If the right's argument is that Tibbetts's murder was preventable because the perpetrator should not have been in the country, then why not find ways to make those other crimes preventable as well? Or are lives less valuable when taken by white American males?

Finally, when Republicans castigate Democrats for bringing up gun control in the immediate aftermath of mass shootings, how do they explain their rush to exploit Mollie Tibbetts's murder? "The same people who say it's always 'too soon' to talk about gun control after a mass shooting are rushing to politicize Mollie Tibbetts' death and call for stricter immigration laws, even though undocumented immigrants are less likely to commit crimes than American citizens," tweeted political consultant Julie Antonellis. "The killer of Mollie Tibbetts killed one person, so Congress *must* act on border wall," wrote Mrs. Betty Bowers, a satirical character created by Andrew Bradley. The Las Vegas mass shooter "killed 58 and wounded 851 in Las Vegas, but Congress *must not* act on guns, because [he] was white. And the NRA paid you to look the other way. Understand now?"

THREE

BATTLE FOR TRUST: DEMOCRACY AND HYPOCRISY

A man becomes trustworthy when you trust him.
—Graham Greene, *The Quiet American*

On August 24, 1855, Abraham Lincoln wrote a letter to his friend Joshua Speed, in which he expressed his contempt for the xenophobic, conspiracy-peddling Know-Nothing movement. "When the Know-Nothings get control," Lincoln wrote, the Declaration of Independence will read "'all men are created equal, except negroes, *and foreigners, and Catholics.*' When it comes to this I should prefer emigrating to some country where they make no pretence of loving liberty—to Russia, for instance, where despotism can be taken pure, and without the base alloy of hypocracy."[1] Lincoln's reference to Russian despotism and right-wing hypocrisy could not be more apt today, when a Republican Party that has traditionally claimed a monopoly on national security capitulated to, covered up, and—in some instances—abetted a Russian cyberattack intended to destabilize the American electoral process.

Russia's strategy in the 2016 presidential campaign was outlined in a declassified 2017 report from the Office of the Director of National Intelligence (ODNI): "We assess Russian President Vladimir Putin ordered an influence campaign in 2016 aimed at the US presidential election. Russia's goals were to undermine public faith in the US democratic process, denigrate Secretary Clinton, and harm her electability and potential presidency. We further assess Putin and the Russian Government developed a clear preference for President-elect Trump."[2] Eighteen months after the ODNI's report was published, Vladimir Putin confirmed the accuracy of the intelligence community's assessment, replying, "Yes, I did," to a question about whether he had backed Trump in 2016.

By any measure, Putin's audacious plan to sabotage Hillary Clinton and boost Donald Trump was a runaway success. On November 8, 2016, Clinton lost the election despite winning the popular vote by 2.1 percent. Russia's interference was not the only factor in Trump's victory—there are a number of reasons why he prevailed over Clinton—but it was an important one. Asked by the *New Yorker*'s Jane Mayer if she thought "Trump would be President without the aid of Russians," Kathleen Hall Jamieson, author of *Cyberwar: How Russian Hackers and Trolls Helped Elect a President*, replied categorically, "No."[3]

NPR detailed the scale and scope of Russia's cyber-intrusion, listing a series of "active measures" against the United States: spies conducting "reconnaissance in several states and cities across the country"; hacking that targeted "more than 500 people or institutions"; and operatives establishing "contact with American political organizations in order to try to wield influence" and possibly forging "documents or other secret material in an attempt to confuse FBI or other intelligence officials at levels only they could see."[4] Russia also targeted U.S. election infrastructure. A CBS *60 Minutes* report identified "a sweeping cyber assault on state voting systems that U.S. intelligence tied to the Russian government."[5] Jeanette Manfra, chief cybersecurity official for the Department of Homeland Security, told NBC News: "We saw a targeting of 21 states and an exceptionally small number of them were actually successfully penetrated."[6]

As social media firms gradually revealed the extent of Russia's infiltration into their networks, the magnitude of the Kremlin's cyberattack became clear. Russia had deployed more than 50,000 bots on Twitter, reached at least 126 million people on Facebook, and targeted voters on platforms from YouTube to Pinterest to Pokémon Go. In October 2018, Twitter made available to the public millions of tweets connected to foreign influence operations, including those from the Internet Research Agency, a Russian troll farm. Technology reporter Nancy Scola analyzed the data and wrote that by Election Day 2016 "the Russian trolls' tweets were nearly uniformly pro-Trump, expressing sentiments like, 'I don't want a criminal in office! I'd vote for Monica before I vote for Killary! #Trump #MakeAmericaGreatAgain #TrumpForPresident.'" Scola pointed out that "Russian accounts appeared to be particularly good at building personality into their tweets."[7] Actor and broadcaster John Fugelsang noted the irony that "the more American flags a profile has, the more likely it's Russian."

A BuzzFeed News analysis found that in the final three months of the 2016 campaign, "the top-performing fake election news stories on Facebook generated more engagement than the top stories from major news outlets such as the *New York Times, Washington Post, Huffington Post,* NBC News, and others."[8] Virtually every one of those fake news stories favored Trump, and as columnist and author Max Boot noted, the vast majority were "either started or spread by Russian bots." Boot, a prominent Never Trumper, scoffed at Republicans who minimized Russia's impact on the election: "Trump and his apologists pretend that the Russian intervention—including the WikiLeaks revelations—was no big deal. That beggars belief."[9] Boot is right: to argue that a highly sophisticated hacking and disinformation campaign targeting tens of millions of voters had no meaningful effect on the election is to defy logic.

"The Russians didn't have to hack election machines, they hacked American minds," said Clint Watts, a former FBI special agent and cybersecurity expert.[10] And they did it with the help of the GOP and the mainstream media. When Trump turned heads by calling on Russia to hack Hillary Clinton's emails—"Russia, if you're listening, I hope you're able to find the 30,000 emails that are missing . . . I think you will probably be rewarded mightily by our press"—Russia quickly did his bidding. Within hours of Trump's request, Kremlin operatives "made their first effort to break into the servers used by Mrs. Clinton's personal office," reported the *New York Times*.[11] Shortly thereafter, according to the *Washington Post*, "the Russians, using an encrypted file with instructions, delivered their trove of hacked emails to WikiLeaks."[12] In 2017, then CIA director Mike Pompeo characterized WikiLeaks as a "non-state hostile intelligence service often abetted by state actors like Russia." Pompeo explained that "Russian military intelligence—the GRU—had used WikiLeaks to release data of U.S. victims that the GRU had obtained through cyber operations against the Democratic National Committee."[13] (Notably, Pompeo, like most Trump supporters, cited WikiLeaks to attack Democrats during the 2016 campaign.)

Just as Trump had predicted, the mainstream media rewarded the Russians for their hack. As soon as WikiLeaks— and DCLeaks, another Russian intelligence front—began dumping stolen Clinton campaign emails online, reporters jumped at the chance to extend their six-hundred-day obsession with Clinton's emails. A *New York Times* investigation concluded that "every major publication, including The Times, published multiple stories citing the D.N.C. and Podesta emails posted by WikiLeaks, becoming a de facto instrument of Russian intelligence."[14] To refer to the national media as a "de facto instrument of Russian intelligence" was a startling admission by the paper of record, one of the rare instances that a major news outlet acknowledged its role in spreading anti-Clinton and pro-Trump propaganda.

And Russia's interference in American elections didn't end in 2016. As ABC News reported, two studies about Russian election interference released at the end of 2018 showed that "rather than slacking off after the 2016 election was over, the online influence operations increased 'substantially,' including a 2017 shift to Instagram that saw in total nearly 200 million 'engagements' on the photo-sharing social media platform."[15] Citing a criminal complaint against a Russian national accused of election meddling, national security reporter Natasha Bertrand noted that Russians had "directed their trolls on social media to call the late Senator John McCain of Arizona an 'old geezer' and Special Counsel Robert Mueller 'a puppet of the establishment.' President Donald Trump, the trolls were told to say, 'deserves a Nobel Peace Prize' for meeting with the North Korean leader Kim Jong Un."[16] Georgetown law professor Joshua Geltzer observed that online discussions on key issues and events "have been polarized, aggravated, and in some instances even driven by Kremlin-backed online influence campaigns." Geltzer concluded that "overall Russia appears to have engaged in more disruptions to democratic dialogue in 2018 than in 2016, not fewer."[17]

Lt. Gen. Mark Hertling and information warfare expert Molly McKew likened Russia's election intrusion to Pearl Harbor and the terrorist attacks of September 11, 2001. Writing in *Politico*, Hertling and McKew argued that America "was targeted by an attack that had different operational objectives and a different overarching strategy, but its aim was every bit as much to devastate the American homeland as Pearl Harbor or 9/11." They noted that "Russian operatives were able to create 'American' personas that interacted freely with American voters, journalists, activists—and campaign officials. They also seemed to have considerable knowledge of how to target and parse American audiences. All of this was subversive and deceptive—but done right out in the open."[18]

Despite the unprecedented scale of the Russian cyber-attack, the GOP's response has been to downplay, deny, and obfuscate. Republican politicians—who have perennially caricatured Democrats and progressives as weak and unpatriotic—all but welcomed Russian intervention because it helped elect a Republican president. And a number of GOP lawmakers went further than mere acquiescence, taking Trump's lead to do the unthinkable: disparage U.S. law enforcement and intelligence agencies to deflect from the Trump campaign's role in the Russian attack. "What's occurring now is as close to Benedict Arnold as I think we're ever going to get in American history," said Malcolm Nance, a popular resistance figure and author of *The Plot to Destroy Democracy: How Putin and His Spies Are Undermining America and Dismantling the West.*[19]

Few of Trump's Capitol Hill defenders were more brazen than former House Intelligence Committee chair Devin Nunes, who was determined to advance a conspiracy theory about a "deep state" out to destroy Trump's presidency. The deep state in this formulation was any current or former government official who opposed Trump, and, specifically, anyone who suggested that Trump's campaign had conspired with Russia to influence the 2016 election. NPR's Geoff Nunberg explained that "depending on the occasion, [the deep state] can encompass the Justice Department, the intelligence communities, the FISA courts, the Democrats and the media."[20]

Nunes's shenanigans were roundly condemned. His hometown newspaper, the *Fresno Bee*, chided him for impugning the integrity of the FBI: "What, pray tell, does Rep. Devin Nunes think he's doing by waving around a secret memo attacking the FBI, the nation's premier law enforcement agency? He certainly isn't representing his Central Valley constituents or Californians, who care much more about health care, jobs and, yes, protecting Dreamers than about the latest conspiracy theory. Instead, he's doing dirty work for House Republican leaders trying to protect President Donald Trump in the Russia investigation."[21] Late-night host Jimmy Kimmel blasted the California congressman and his GOP cohorts, saying, "This is how our government works now: If your party is in charge, you can lie, you can cheat, you can game the system to benefit your buddies . . . To call Devin Nunes Donald Trump's lap dog would be an insult to dogs. And laps."[22]

Nunes wasn't alone in his dogged determination to play defense for Trump and Russia. Even after losing control of the House in the 2018 midterms, the outgoing Republican majority rushed to use its expiring subpoena power to sow confusion about special counsel Robert Mueller's Russia investigation. Rep. Jerrold Nadler, the ranking Democrat on the Judiciary

Committee, denounced the subpoenas sent to former attorney general Loretta Lynch and former FBI director James Comey as "coming out of the blue, with very little time left on the calendar, and after the American people have resoundingly rejected the GOP's approach to oversight—if, indeed, 'oversight' is the word we should use for running interference for President Trump."[23]

Emboldened by the zealousness of his Republican defenders, Trump openly obstructed the Mueller investigation, firing FBI director James Comey in 2017 and attorney general Jeff Sessions in 2018, both times admitting his decision was related to the Russia probe. And GOP leaders continued to undercut Mueller and circle the wagons around Trump. On three occasions, Senate majority leader Mitch McConnell blocked a bill protecting Mueller's investigation. "Nixon wished for friends like these," tweeted Walter Shaub, former head of the Office of Government Ethics.

Trump's GOP-approved rampages against the FBI and Justice Department stood in marked contrast to his unvarnished praise for Russian president Vladimir Putin. A July 2018 meeting between the two heads of state in Helsinki, Finland, was dubbed the "Treason Summit" after Trump defended Russia and denigrated U.S. intelligence and law enforcement agencies. Trump's sycophancy toward Putin at the post-summit press conference sparked a national outcry, prompting former CIA director John Brennan to tweet, "Donald Trump's press conference performance in Helsinki rises to & exceeds the threshold of 'high crimes & misdemeanors.' It was nothing short of treasonous. Not only were Trump's comments imbecilic, he is wholly in the pocket of Putin. Republican Patriots: Where are you???" (Brennan was subsequently stripped of security clearance by the White House.)

Washington Post columnist Ruth Marcus called on White House aides to resign in protest. "Everyone who works for Trump: quit now," Marcus tweeted. "Save your souls. Save your honor. Save your reputation. Russia attacked our democracy. He doesn't care, won't defend our country." Former presidential adviser David Gergen, typically a measured commentator, posted a scathing tweet questioning Trump's patriotism: "The fact that Trump chose a thug over the American people and his own officials captures just how unpresidential and unpatriotic he is. Never have I seen a president so badly betray his own country on the world stage."

W. Kamau Bell, host of CNN's *United Shades of America*, framed Trump's historic capitulation in matter-of-fact terms: "If you had a day at work like the day @realDonaldTrump had today, security would be at your office waiting for you, asking for your key card, w/ all your possessions in a box, & a cup for you to pee in." Author Susan Bordo tweeted her disbelief that "this treason can possibly be normalized by the GOP & that the media will gasp & sputter & preach and then move on." Even Fox News host Neil Cavuto called Trump's subservient behavior at the Helsinki summit "disgusting."

But the Republican Party wasn't about to stand up to

Trump (or Putin). While a number of GOP officials grumbled about the shameful spectacle in Helsinki, Axios reported that "almost every elected Republican we talk to privately thinks President Trump's warm embrace of Vladimir Putin was unexplainable, unacceptable and un-American. Yes, they wish they could say this publicly. No, they won't—not now, and probably never."[24] If Axios was right, and Republican leaders were mortified by Trump's behavior, they concealed it well. Mike Pence—described by conservative columnist George Will as "oleaginous" and with a "talent for toady-ism"—declared: "Our POTUS is now on his way home from a historic trip to Europe . . . the world saw once again that President Trump stands without apology as the leader of the free world."[25]

Reacting to Pence's remarks, Twitter user Daisy McDonald exclaimed, "Good God. How far down the chain of succession do we have to go before we land on someone who is not a straight up traitor?" As if to answer her question, Ohio reporter Jeremy Pelzer snapped a photo of two MAGA-capped white males at a Trump rally wearing shirts emblazoned with the words "I'd rather be Russian than Democrat." Reporter Zack Beauchamp commented that the photo was one of those images "that so perfectly encapsulate a moment in time that all you can do is marvel. They're the kinds of things that will show up in history textbooks, the kind of thing that high school students will look at when they're trying to understand a previous era." Beauchamp described the image as "an extremely clear way of understanding how deep hatred of Democrats is warping the Republican Party, part of a phenomenon political scientists call 'negative partisanship.'"[26] Or, in common parlance, "owning the libs," a phrase that has come to represent the right's penchant for self-destructive behavior intended to spite the left. "Trump's base is ready to renounce U.S. citizenship to own the libs," tweeted investigative journalist Julia Davis.

"The end of America First," said journalist Garance Franke-Ruta of the pro-Russia MAGA photo. "The party of which I was a member my entire life has been taken over by traitors," wrote Twitter user Nicholas Kile. Former federal prosecutor and CNN analyst Renato Mariotti laid the blame squarely on the GOP leadership: "Republicans, your failure to stand up to Trump's disinformation campaign caused this. The end result would make Putin proud—Americans proudly choosing Russia over their fellow Americans." Digital activist Ryan Knight tweeted that Trump had "publicly asked Russia to commit the crime & hack Hillary's emails. He publicly confessed he fired Comey b/c of Russia. He publicly sided w/ Putin over US Intelligence. He publicly attacks FBI & Mueller. Trump's publicly telling us he is a TRAITOR. When will America listen?"

Blue America *was* listening. But red America was impervious to patriotic appeals. Between 2014 and 2018, the percentage of Republicans who considered Russia an ally or "friendly" shot *up* from 22 percent to 40 percent. Trump's stubborn defense of Putin hadn't deterred his party; to the contrary, nearly 70 percent of Republicans approved of how Trump handled the Helsinki summit according to a CBS News poll, and a solid majority of Republicans were unconcerned about Russian efforts to interfere in future elections.[27] The so-called "real Americans" of the GOP base were now acting as Russian appeasers, bolstering Trump as he attacked U.S. law enforcement and intelligence agencies to cover for Putin. "What happened to the Republican Party?" asked former president Barack Obama. "Its central organizing principle in foreign policy was the fight against Communism, and now they're cozying up to the former head of the KGB, actively blocking legislation that would defend our elections from Russian attack. What happened?"[28] The answer, according to political strategist Brad Bannon, was that the Grand Old Party had become "a wholly owned subsidiary of the Trump Organization."[29]

Republicans argued that the Obama administration's Russia sanctions had *toughened* under Trump, and that Obama's inadequate response to the Russian election attack was the *real* scandal. But it was clear from the Helsinki summit that GOP leaders would do nothing of substance to address Trump's humiliating deference to the Russian leader. In effect, Putin would get away with his cyberassault. Russian aggression would not be met with a clear and forceful rebuttal from the U.S. After decades of tarnishing liberals as traitors, red America was waving the white flag: the GOP's "real American" patriots had surrendered to a hostile adversary's attack on American democracy, ignoring it, minimizing it, and even turning on U.S. intelligence and law enforcement communities to deny it. Ronald Reagan was lionized by Republicans for commanding the Soviets to "tear down this wall," but his party was now sheepishly accepting an act of cyberwar by a Russian spymaster. "GOP = Giving Ourselves to Putin," tweeted Democratic strategist Paul Begala. Tribalism had trumped patriotism.

A Redditor named "TheDVille" took aim at the GOP's traitorous behavior: "Republicans were given the option to defend America from foreign attacks, or defend the man who actively invited them. They chose Trump. It's clear that Trump does not stand for the country and the people he is supposed to represent. Republicans brand themselves as Patriots, and denounce anyone who stands in their way as anti-American. They should never be able to call themselves Patriots again, without having to answer for their action during this time." The Republican Party's hypocrisy on Russia—claiming to be patriots and defenders of the flag while surrendering to Putin—is part of their pattern of treating hypocrisy not as a source of shame but as a tool of ideological warfare. This conspicuous lack of principle has been a major factor in the rise of the Never Trump movement. Steve Schmidt, who served as a senior strategist to the late Sen. John McCain, quit the Republican Party, stating that it was "filled with feckless cowards who disgrace and dishonor the legacies of the party's greatest leaders." Schmidt said the GOP was now "a danger to our democracy and values."

No politician embodies the Republican Party's moral

cratering more than South Carolina senator Lindsey Graham, whose about-face from Trump critic to slobbering fan led MSNBC host Ari Melber to say that Graham had descended "into pure self-caricature of craven political hypocrisy" and that he had "come to personify the hollowing out of a significant portion of the leadership of the Republican Party." Melber took Graham to task for his blatant contradictions on Trump. "I think he's a kook. I think he's crazy," Graham said of Trump in 2016, only to claim, two and a half years later, that Trump "deserves the Nobel Peace Prize and then some." "And then some," Melber repeated, noting that Graham had "abandoned his own publicly stated, repeated convictions in exchange for what looks like, now, a certain proximity to being with Trump."[30]

Graham's reversals are dizzying: In 2017, he warned there would be "holy hell to pay" if Trump fired attorney general Jeff Sessions. When Trump did exactly that, Graham timidly said, "I look forward to working with President Trump to find a confirmable, worthy successor so that we can start a new chapter at the Department of Justice." Confronted with his contradiction by a Fox News host, Graham laughed. "So, when was that?" he asked. "What year?"[31]

At the confirmation hearings for Supreme Court justice Brett Kavanaugh—accused of sexual assault by three women, and of perjury by much of the political world—Graham admonished Democrats, "If you want to pick judges from your way of thinking, then you better win an election." To which Irin Carmon, coauthor of the bestselling *Notorious RBG: The Life and Times of Ruth Bader Ginsburg*, responded, "Hadn't @BarackObama won when Scalia died?" Steve Benen of *MaddowBlog* elaborated: "Well, Barack Obama won an election—in fact, he won two—and when he tried to fill a Supreme Court vacancy with a compromise nominee recommended by Republicans, Graham and his GOP colleagues refused to even give Merrick Garland a hearing." Benen continued, "If 'winning an election' is the prerequisite to picking judges, why did Graham participate in a partisan scheme to steal a Supreme Court seat from a democratically elected president?"[32]

On Facebook, Michael Moore (not the filmmaker) posted about Graham's rank hypocrisy: "If I had to create a list of the most pathetic Republican lawmakers, I wouldn't know where to start. However, I can say with certainty that Lindsey Graham would be near the top of the list. The manner in which he has kissed up to tRump [capitalizing the 'R' in Trump is an intentional misspelling to convey disrespect] has been a prime example of a man who has been stripped of character, dignity, and self-respect. He, along with his cohorts, will go down in history as co-conspirators to tRump's attempt to destroy American democracy."

When Trump replaced Attorney General Sessions with Matthew Whitaker—who had publicly expressed skepticism of the Mueller investigation and was facing widespread calls to recuse himself from the probe—Graham told CBS News:

"I think he was appropriately appointed legally. I don't think he has to recuse himself."[33] In response, *Lawfare* executive editor Susan Hennessey tweeted, "There is no depth to which Graham will not sink in his groveling debasement before this administration. What an absolute disgrace."

Splinter News's Rafi Schwartz wrote disdainfully of Graham, "There's no one else in Washington who crams quite as much unadulterated bullshit into such a small frame."[34] But Graham had competition in the person of Mitch McConnell. *Esquire*'s Charles P. Pierce opined that "There simply is no more loathsome creature walking the political landscape than the Majority Leader of the United States Senate."[35] After Democrats regained control of the House, McConnell posed a query on Twitter: "Will Dems work with us, or simply put partisan politics ahead of the country?" McConnell's tweet was promptly "ratioed off the internet," in the words of the Daily Dot, garnering more than ten times as many (negative) comments as retweets. McConnell had spent eight years obstructing Barack Obama's agenda; he had orchestrated the theft of a Supreme Court pick from America's first black president; he had blocked attempts to get to the bottom of Russia's cyberattack; and he had abandoned his constitutionally mandated oversight duties in order to empower Donald Trump. In 2016, McConnell boasted to his constituents, "One of my proudest moments was when I looked at Barack Obama in the eye and I said, 'Mr. President, you will not fill this Supreme Court vacancy.'" Now he was calling on Democrats to place "partisan politics ahead of the country." A Twitter user named Sharon Allen slammed McConnell: "If hypocrisy was asphalt, you would pave from D.C. to Anchorage!"

Accusations of hypocrisy are ubiquitous in American politics, and there is plenty of hypocrisy to go around. Many Democrats who criticized George W. Bush for violating civil liberties went silent when Barack Obama continued—and in some cases, expanded—Bush's policies on indefinite detention, drone strikes, and extrajudicial killings. Democrats who maintain that women should be believed when they come forward with accusations of sexual assault have been reluctant to say the same about former president Bill Clinton's accusers. That said, the GOP has taken hypocrisy to new extremes, shedding all pretense of consistency or honesty. "Part of being a hypocrite is that you don't care when people point out your hypocrisy," tweeted "FlamingLib," a progressive activist.

The Republican Party's hypocrisy is part of a larger right-wing assault on the bonds of trust between citizens, media, and government. Truth for Republican politicians is now whatever they say it is, even if it contradicts statements made a year, a month, or a day before. When Trump said "there's no proof of anything," he was describing the GOP's increasingly tenuous relationship to reality. Flagrant contradictions are more than just slipups or gaffes for Republican politicians; they have become the essence of the Republican Party's message. The irony, as the novelist Kurt Andersen pointed out, is that "the American right has insistently decried the spread of relativism, the idea that nothing is any more correct or true than anything else."[36] Which is why "conservative" should be used sparingly to describe the modern GOP, a far-right party that has nothing to do with principled conservatism.

FOUR

BATTLE FOR JUSTICE: THE NEW PATRIOT

Patriotism embraces dissent. It places the overarching values of the country over the short-term interests of the party; it is a child of hope.
—Rev. Byron Williams

On Independence Day 2018, the right-wing website Power Line published "Why Do Democrats Hate America?," a post that opened with a sweeping statement: "It is common knowledge that patriotic Americans tend to be Republicans, while unpatriotic Americans tend to be Democrats." The author, John Hinderaker, complained that "the college-educated and the young are the least proud to be Americans. This is the result of a generation of mis-education, in which Howard Zinn has become the #1 guide to American history and Karl Marx is far more widely taught than John Locke."[1] Hinderaker based his argument on a Gallup poll that asked respondents if they were proud to be American. It did not ask whether their pride was demonstrated through actions that upheld the nation's ideals and principles. When it comes to defining patriotism, the distinction matters.

For Democrats and progressives, patriotism is based on values, and values on actions that reflect America's highest aspirations. Political theorist John Schaar described this form of patriotism as "love of one's own land and people, love too of the best ideals of one's own culture and tradition." It is the patriotism of principle and purpose, of matching moral goals to moral deeds. "Jefferson spoke for it, as did Lincoln and Martin Luther King Jr," Schaar wrote.[2]

Because Republican politicians often use patriotism and nationalism interchangeably, accurate definitions are important. "The difference between patriotism and nationalism is that the patriot is proud of his country for what it does, and the nationalist is proud of his country no matter what it does; the first attitude creates a feeling of responsibility, but the second a feeling of blind arrogance that leads to war," wrote author and syndicated columnist Sydney J. Harris.[3] Political cartoonist Jen Sorensen framed patriotism simply as "pride in who you are," and nationalism as "pride in who you aren't."[4]

George Orwell, whose name has become synonymous with the post-2016 era, wrote that patriotism is "devotion to a particular place and a particular way of life, which one believes to be the best in the world but has no wish to force on other people." By contrast, Orwell argued, nationalism is "the habit of identifying oneself with a single nation or other unit, placing it beyond good and evil and recognizing no other duty than that of advancing its interests." With characteristic insight, Orwell wrote that the nationalist "sees history, especially contemporary history, as the endless rise and decline of great power units, and every event that happens seems to him a demonstration that his own side is on the up-grade and some hated rival is on the down-grade."[5]

A robust conception of patriotism is grounded in behavior, not belief. Theodore Roosevelt defined it as fealty to the nation, not fanaticism about a leader, stating, "Patriotism means to stand by the country. It does not mean to stand by the president or any other public official, save exactly to the degree in which he himself stands by the country."[6] A century later, Roosevelt's words serve as a warning to Trump apologists, who have supported the abuse of asylum-seeking children, the facilitation of a Russian cyberassault on U.S. democracy, the smearing of the FBI, and effusive praise for enemies and tyrants—all while wrapping themselves in the flag. These actions are antithetical to the most rudimentary notion of American patriotism. True patriots feel no pride when their nation's leaders violate fundamental democratic norms and standards.

The divergence between Republicans and Democrats on patriotism hinges on their differing views of dissent. "Democrats are more likely than Republicans to believe that patriotism can include dissent," wrote Nathaniel Rakich and Dhrumil Mehta in an article for polling analysis site FiveThirtyEight. Rakich and Mehta reported that a year after the September 11 attacks "93 percent of Democrats and

99 percent of Republicans said they were either 'extremely' or 'very' proud to be Americans. By January 2007, amid an unpopular war in Iraq that sparked no small amount of liberal dissent, the share of Democrats who were 'extremely' or 'very' proud to be Americans had shrunk to 74 percent."[7] That number plummeted further after Donald Trump took office.

The partisan battle over patriotism came to a head in the summer of 2016, when San Francisco 49ers quarterback Colin Kaepernick refused to stand during the national anthem. "I am not going to stand up to show pride in a flag for a country that oppresses black people and people of color," Kaepernick said.[8] Other athletes soon joined Kaepernick, kneeling or sitting during the anthem to oppose police brutality and racial injustice. Megan Garber, a staff writer at the *Atlantic*, tracked the expanding protests: "Terrell Suggs took a knee. Leonard Fournette took a knee. At a game played in London on Sunday afternoon, many of their fellow Ravens and Jaguars took a knee. Before the Lions met the Falcons in Detroit on Sunday, Rico LaVelle sang 'The Star-Spangled Banner.' And then he took a knee."[9] The protests quickly became a cultural flashpoint, separating those who argued that kneeling—a universal gesture of reverence—was a patriotic form of protest, and those who claimed that refusing to stand during the anthem was an insult to the flag and the military.

Combat veteran Kate Logan tweeted, "Because protest IS patriotic. I wouldn't defend a country that stood, or kneeled, for anything less." Civil rights leader Rev. Dr. William Barber said the "NFL players who #TakeAKnee are sons of Justice, taking their place in the river of resistance that has brought us thus far on our way." Twitter user "Canada Hates Trump" wrote sarcastically, "I get why people are mad at Kaepernick. Isn't he the guy who sexually assaulted 19 women, sided with Putin over America's own intelligence agencies, tossed paper towels in the aftermath of a hurricane, called African countries shitholes & called Kim Jong-Un a very honorable man?" Writer Mychal Denzel Smith put it succinctly: "Kaepernick refused to participate in the compulsory patriotism ordered by the NFL."[10]

The #TakeAKnee movement was met with anger and indignation on the right. The right-wing YouTube channel USA Breaking News posted a video titled "The Awesome Thing Happening to Ungrateful NFL Players Who 'Take a Knee' During the Anthem." The clip gloated over sagging NFL ratings and referred to the "self-entitled, misguided, uninformed" Kaepernick. YouTube commenter Walter Ferres agreed: "These steaming piles of pig feces known as football players, are destroying the NFL platform by lying and saying the reason they are taking the knee is because of police brutality against black criminals that deserve to be beat or killed for the crimes they commit." But #TakeAKnee isn't about black criminals. It is about black *victims* of police brutality and racial injustice, among them Philando Castile, Oscar Grant, Sandra Bland, Eric Garner, and twelve-year-old Tamir Rice—who was shot by police in a Cleveland park and ignored by them as he lay dying in the snow.

Rice's heartbreaking and infuriating story illustrates precisely why #TakeAKnee is necessary, because we continue to "see that the constitutional rights of Black Americans are not recognized by the legal system," as human rights activist Bree Newsome tweeted. On November 22, 2014, a man called 911 and told a dispatcher that a male, "probably a juvenile," was brandishing a pistol, which was "probably fake." "He's sitting on a swing right now . . . he's probably a juvenile," the caller repeated. The dispatcher asked whether the individual holding the gun was black or white three times, confirmed he was black, then reportedly failed to convey to the dispatched police unit that the person being reported was most likely a boy holding a fake gun.

What followed was effectively a drive-by shooting. Surveillance video captured a police cruiser pulling up to Rice, and one of two responding officers—who had been deemed unfit for duty at a previous police department—gunning down the twelve-year-old at point-blank range within two seconds of arriving. As Rice lay mortally wounded on the snowy ground, the officers refused to administer first aid. Four minutes later, an FBI agent investigating a nearby crime attended to Rice as the responding officers stood and watched. When Rice's young sister ran toward her dying brother, she was roughed up by police. According to HuffPost, "Surveillance footage . . . shows authorities forcing the young victim's 14-year-old sister to the ground, handcuffing her and putting her in a patrol car."[11] Cleveland's deputy police chief later indicated that Tamir Rice "did not threaten the officer verbally or physically," Cleveland.com reported.[12]

An Ohio grand jury declined to indict the officers. Journalist Steven W. Thrasher wrote that the problem was "America's irrational fear of black boys."[13] *New Yorker* writer Jelani Cobb explained that "skin is a uniform, too," and that "police tend to significantly overestimate the age and dismiss the potential innocence of black youths."[14] Writer and activist Jamilah Lemieux said, simply, that "Tamir Rice was, and still is, almost unspeakable."[15]

In her book *Unbought and Unbossed*, trailblazing congress-woman Shirley Chisholm wrote, "'Liberty and justice for all' were beautiful words, but the ugly fact was that liberty and justice were only for white males."[16] And for Tamir Rice, there was no justice—killed for holding a toy while black, left to die on the sidewalk, his distraught sister manhandled, and his killers facing no legal consequences. *That* is why athletes protest during the national anthem. As educator and organizer Brittany Packnett tweeted, "We out here depending on camera phones and strangers to stay alive. In 2018. That ain't freedom."

Like most political battles in the U.S., public opinion on #TakeAKnee has broken along racial lines. Investigative reporter Kathryn Casteel noted sharp differences "between what black and white Americans say is the protests' purpose." Among white respondents, Casteel reported, "50 percent said players were trying to disrespect the flag," while just "11 percent of black respondents said the same."[17] Brandeis University professor Chad Williams wrote that the furious opposition to the protests reflects "what happens when African-Americans physically and symbolically challenge an understanding of patriotism rooted in white supremacy and racist ideas of black subservience." When the NFL announced a policy that required players on the sideline to stand—but offered them the option to remain in the locker room—Williams argued that the NFL "acquiesced to the threats of President Trump and the unrest of its white fan base by establishing a policy that requires black players to remain docile, obedient employees, devoid of any outward expression of racial and political consciousness, which sole purpose is to entertain and enrich their owners."[18]

Researcher Martenzie Johnson examined the precedents for #TakeAKnee. "Boxer Muhammad Ali refused induction into the U.S. Army in 1967, was stripped of his world title and had his New York State Athletic Commission boxing title revoked. Ali wasn't revered as a civil rights leader by the public at large until he lost the ability to speak," Johnson wrote. "Olympic sprinters John Carlos and Tommie Smith won gold and bronze medals for the United States at the 1968 Olympic Games, raised their black-gloved fists as The Star-Spangled Banner was played, and were expelled by the International Olympic Committee," he added.[19]

The history of the national anthem sheds light on the current battle over #TakeAKnee. Francis Scott Key, who wrote the lyrics of "The Star-Spangled Banner," owned slaves, and his rarely sung third verse includes the lines, "No refuge could save the hireling and slave / From the terror of flight or the gloom of the grave." "The Star-Spangled Banner" wasn't officially recognized as America's national anthem until 1931. During the twentieth century, a number of changes were made to the code of conduct required during performances of the anthem—a code that comes with no legal penalties. Today, 36 U.S.C. § 171 reads:

> During rendition of the national anthem when the flag is displayed, all present except those in uniform should stand at attention facing the flag with the right hand over the heart. Men not in uniform should remove their headdress with their right hand and hold it at the left shoulder, the hand being over the heart. Persons in uniform should render the military salute at the first note of the anthem and retain this position until the last note. When the flag is not displayed, those present should face toward the music and act in the same manner they would if the flag were displayed there.[20]

All of which is to say that a citizen's behavior during the playing of the national anthem is a codified convention, one that has evolved over the decades. By exercising their free-speech rights to oppose injustice during renditions of the anthem, athletes are working within that convention, enriching our understanding of our flag and our identity. "A piece of cloth is not sacred, and a song (especially one with a suspect genesis) is not sacred," wrote pastor and digital activist John Pavlovitz. "They are symbols of a freedom that those serving our country have died to give all of us and to protect for all of us." Pavlovitz admonished #TakeAKnee opponents: "By creating a black and white 'Traitorous NFL Player vs. America' storyline, you're able to completely ignore the stated and repeated impetus behind Kaepernick's initial protest (and every one that's followed): the plea for people of color to be treated with equity by law enforcement, the criminal justice system, and our government. When the President labels these men 'sons of bitches' who should be terminated—he's only proving why their protests are valid and necessary to begin with."[21]

Communications strategist Ana Blinder, who worked for the NFL and saw #TakeAKnee unfold from the inside, wrote about the careful consideration that had gone into the protests, pointing out that the athletes "were never protesting the military, but rather racial injustice—police brutality, mass incarceration, and systemic racism. I've heard this from them directly. They were pointed and thoughtful about their motives."[22] Nate Boyer, the Green Beret who first advised Kaepernick to kneel, explained that he suggested kneeling "because people kneel to pray; we'll kneel in front of a fallen brother's grave." In October 2017, Boyer wrote a heartfelt open letter to all Americans, appealing for unity: "I'm laying it all out there because I have to, I swore to defend this land and its people, and I will die trying. I know some people will hate this (we love to hate things these days), and I'll get called a disgrace to the Green Beret once again. But I don't care, the United States means more to me than any of that."[23]

But for Republicans conditioned to claim sole possession of America's national symbols, there was no room for nuance or civility. #TakeAKnee was a call to arms. Self-avowed nationalist Donald Trump led the charge: "First time kneeling, out for game. Second time kneeling, out for season/no pay!" Recalling his *The Apprentice* punch line, Trump tweeted, "Get that son of a bitch off the field right now. Out! He's fired. He's fired!"

Charlie Kirk, a young Republican once described by the *Dallas Morning News* as a leader of "the Trump campaign's millennial assault," tweeted, "These protests aren't about [police brutality], they're about hating America and hating Trump." On Facebook, writer Anne Carden launched a tirade against NFL players, exclaiming, "THE NEXT TIME YOU, THE UNGRATEFUL, DECIDE TO TAKE A KNEE INSTEAD OF SALUTING OUR FLAG AND HONORING THIS GREAT COUNTRY, I INVITE YOU TO WATCH THIS VIDEO [on U.S. prisoners of war] AND LEARN WHAT TRUE PATRIOTISM IS REALLY ABOUT."

When Nike chose Colin Kaepernick to be the face of a new advertising campaign, Kaepernick's detractors were enraged. "Good to know Nike supports an 'oppressed' crybaby who hates America," tweeted Fox Nation host Tomi Lahren. *Esquire's* Jonathan Evans poked fun at the Nike critics: "Some folks who conflate the player protests against social ills in

America with just plain hating America/the flag/the national anthem (pick one) got very angry! And so they started destroying their own Nike gear. With fire . . . This is both amazing and incredibly stupid. Amazing because, well . . . *people are, with no apparent sense of irony or self-awareness, lighting stuff they paid for on fire and calling it a boycott.* That's also the reason it's incredibly stupid. Boycotting is supposed to be a means of putting economic pressure on a company."[24]

Russian trolls and bots soon joined the action. ABC News reported that "Russian internet trolls are trying to stoke the controversy in the U.S. over NFL players kneeling during the national anthem by using opposing hashtags such as #TakeAKnee and #BoycottNFL."[25] The news media muddied the issue further by repeatedly mischaracterizing the athletes' dissent as protests against the anthem. Center for American Progress president Neera Tanden corrected the record: "THEY ARE NOT PROTESTING THE NATIONAL ANTHEM. They are protesting police brutality." Saying NFL players are protesting the anthem is like saying "hunger strikes are against food," tweeted comedian Orli Matlow.

#TakeAKnee was a point of contention in the Texas Senate race between Democratic congressman Beto O'Rourke and incumbent GOP senator (and Trump apologist) Ted Cruz. Responding to a veteran's question about the protests, O'Rourke delivered an expansive, well-reasoned defense of the kneeling athletes, lauding "peaceful, nonviolent protest including taking a knee at a football game to point out that black men, unarmed, black teenagers, unarmed, and black children, unarmed, are being killed at a frightening level right now, including by law enforcement, without accountability and without justice."[26] The video of O'Rourke's widely praised comments racked up tens of millions of views across Facebook, Twitter, Instagram, Snapchat, and YouTube. Basketball superstar LeBron James called the clip a "must watch." Director Ava DuVernay tweeted, "Solid way to start your morning if you believe in justice and dignity for all. I'm keeping an eye on this guy."

O'Rourke had struck a nerve, and Ted Cruz retaliated by releasing a campaign ad called "Stand for the Anthem," which featured a Vietnam veteran saying, "I gave two legs for this country. I'm not able to stand. But I sure expect you to stand for me when the national anthem is being played."[27] Cruz hammered O'Rourke at a press conference: "We need to be respectful of our active-duty military. We need to be respectful of our veterans. We need to be respectful of law enforcement as well." On Twitter, Cruz defaulted to a standard GOP trope: "Most Texans stand for the flag, but Hollywood liberals are so excited that Beto is siding with NFL players protesting the national anthem that Kevin Bacon just retweeted it."

The battle between Cruz and O'Rourke over #TakeAKnee was a proxy for the larger red-blue fight over American identity, the struggle to define the "real American." Cruz's reference to Hollywood liberals was an effort to paint O'Rourke as an unpatriotic elitist whose values were out of sync with the "true patriots" of the heartland. But if respect for the military is a litmus test for patriots, as Republicans like Ted Cruz insist it is, the GOP has failed miserably. Taking Trump's lead, Republican politicians have smeared veterans and Gold Star families who pose a political threat, including Robert Mueller, John Kerry, Tammy Duckworth, and the parents of decorated army captain Humayun Khan, killed in action during the Iraq war. The Khans were hounded by Trump and his MAGA voters during the 2016 campaign.

National security reporter Nicole Gaouette wrote that Trump "insulted war heroes, prisoners of war, Gold Star families and, some critics say, tried to use the troops to score political points. He's directed 5% cuts at Veterans Affairs, which for some time he left in the control of non-veterans who happened to be members of his Mar-a-Lago club. He's . . . passed up Veterans Day ceremonies other leaders made time to attend and repeatedly said he knows more about military issues than generals do."[28] Asked by the Associated Press why he hadn't been to a combat zone, Trump replied, "Well, I will do that at some point, but I don't think it's overly necessary. I've been very busy with everything that's taking place here."[29] Digital activist Jennifer Hayden tweeted in response, "Since he took office, Donald Trump has found 149 days for golf."

Under intense criticism, Trump finally paid a Christmas visit to troops in Iraq two years into his term. But as journalist Ayman Mohyeldin pointed out, "Pres Trump spent 3 hours in Iraq: 1) lied about 10% pay increase to troops 2) revealed classified identity of Navy SEALs 3) possibly violated rules against political activity on a military base 4) broke protocol by a visiting head of state by not going to meet Iraqi PM." Retired rear admiral John Kirby weighed in on Trump's Iraq trip, tweeting, "One of the reasons I wince when Trump spends time with troops. They're excited to see him. They deserve the attention. But they don't deserve to have their service politicized. They are not a MAGA crowd. If Trump really respected them, he would leave partisanship back in DC."

In November 2018, reports surfaced about veterans being stiffed out of reimbursements they were owed under the "Forever" GI Bill. According to *Stars and Stripes*, "Part of the new GI Bill changed how veterans' housing allowances are calculated—they're now supposed to be based on where veterans take classes, rather than defaulting to their school's main campus. The change was supposed to be made by Aug. 1, 2018, but information technology problems have set back implementation to Dec. 1, 2019."[30] MSNBC political analyst Elise Jordan asked, "And why is this not a number one priority of the Trump administration? They said they were going to be all about taking care of vets and they're just gonna let this stand? Because of their own incompetency?" Jordan continued, "I'm so sick of the platitudes about support our troops, support our troops. Paul Ryan talking about the men and women who served in Iraq and Afghanistan . . . let's figure out what we're actually doing in a place like Afghanistan where yesterday a U.S. bomb killed 30 civilians. That would actually be taking care of our troops."

One of the most conspicuous examples of the right's

selective support for the troops is the unseemly treatment of the late Sen. John McCain, whose final days were marred by petty White House posturing and malicious smears by right-wing detractors. When the White House initially refused to fly the flag at half-staff following McCain's death, retired four-star general Michael Hayden tweeted a photo of the White House with the flag flying at full staff against the backdrop of the Washington Monument. "Remember this image the next time this President talks about disrespecting veterans," Hayden wrote.

Days before McCain's passing, GOP strategist Rick Wilson—dubbed the Never Trump movement's godfather—blasted commenters on Breitbart News for mercilessly attacking the senator as he lay on his deathbed: "If you were looking for the goddamn abyss of Trumpian depravity, go read the comments on the Breitbart article about McCain ending his cancer treatment. The garbage that run that site lack a shred of decency and those commenters are human filth." One commenter, "proreason," wrote that McCain's "contempt for Americans who disagree with him is disgusting. Thank God that the nightmare of his 'service' is finally coming to an end."

McCain's policies and positions were debatable to some, objectionable to others, but there is no question that he was the kind of public figure typically lionized by red America, a navy pilot who endured years of torture and nearly gave his life for his country. But in the end, this lifelong Republican was treated with more respect by Democrats than by his own party. McCain's favorable rating at his death was nearly twenty points higher among Democrats than Republicans, his unfavorables among Democrats twenty points lower. It wasn't a liberal politician who ridiculed McCain's years as a prisoner of war; it was right-wing favorite Donald Trump who said, "He's not a war hero . . . I like people that weren't captured." And it was Republican voters who elected Trump commander in chief despite that disqualifying insult to a decorated veteran.

Trump's attacks on members of the military prompted Brandon Friedman, a former Obama administration official who served in the U.S. Army, to post a photo of the Situation Room on the night Osama bin Laden was killed overlaid with derogatory Trump tweets about officials in the room. The effect is jarring. A roomful of U.S. leaders overseeing a historic military operation tagged with juvenile insults from a sitting president. It is difficult to envision a reasonable conception of American patriotism that includes a president taunting and besmirching the people who helped bring the 9/11 mastermind to justice.

Particularly abhorrent was the ease with which Trump and his Republican enablers vilified retired navy admiral William H. McRaven, the special operations commander who oversaw bin Laden's killing. VoteVets, a political organization that focuses on veterans' issues, voiced outrage that the GOP was "backing smears against a man who did nothing but dedicate 37 years of his life to defending America, organizing and overseeing the mission to take out one of our most dangerous foes in the process. Disgusting. Absolutely disgusting." Former GOP communications director Tara Setmayer argued that "Trump, a draft dodging coward, doesn't love or respect our military. He uses them as political props. Trump's petulant response here disrespects the service of Adm. McRaven & countless other special ops heroes who serve honorably daily, despite politics. Just despicable." Attorney and former senior Obama aide Ronald Klain tweeted, "May 1, 2011: John Brennan was in the Sit Room overseeing the mission against Bin Laden—which he had planned and kept secret for months. Admiral McRaven was in command of that mission. And where was Donald Trump?" To answer the question, Klain shared a screenshot of the shooting schedule for an episode of *The Apprentice*.

Trump's first tweet of 2019 was a broadside against retired four-star army general Stanley McChrystal: "'General' McChrystal got fired like a dog by Obama. Last assignment a total bust. Known for big, dumb mouth. Hillary lover!" McChrystal had criticized Trump, and as CNN reporter Jim Sciutto pointed out, "Military heroism and sacrifice is no protection if you criticize Trump." Fred Wellman, a veteran of four Iraq combat tours, tweeted, "If you think that smearing McChrystal or any of the generals will turn the hardcore Trump loving veterans and military people against him you need to stop. They won't. If you speak out against Trump you're an 'oath breaker' to these robots."

Democratic activists regularly ponder what would happen if Barack Obama or Hillary Clinton had treated the flag and the military with the same disrespect as have Trump and his GOP apologists. And after Trump's fawning summit with murderous North Korean dictator Kim Jong-un, even controversial right-wing blogger Erick Erickson saw fit to make the comparison: "President Trump should not have engaged in a glad-handing, face time exercise with the North Korean leader where the communist monster gets a propaganda win of North Korean flags at equal display with the American flag . . . Had Barack Obama done that, Republicans would be demanding his impeachment."[31]

The Republican Party's hypocrisy on patriotism isn't limited to attacks on decorated veterans. Its embrace of right-wing extremism has made red America a breeding ground for white supremacists, anti-Semites, and neo-Nazis, the very hatemongers that the Greatest Generation sacrificed life and limb to defeat. Political commentator Ana Navarro tweeted that "pedophiles, convicts, racists, bigots, Neo-Nazis are all choosing to run as Republicans. Worse yet, they are actually mounting credible campaigns and getting support. It should worry any Republican left with an iota of decency." Yale law professor Scott Shapiro tweeted sarcastically, "'Daddy, why are so many Republicans Nazis now?' 'Well, son, it's the Democrats' fault. They wanted health care for poor people.'"

You can't simultaneously "support the troops" and embolden the enemies of American democracy. Nor can you claim ownership of the flag if you are more outraged by athletes protesting injustice than by injustice itself. On Thanksgiving

Day 2018, Alabama police shot and killed twenty-one-year-old E. J. Bradford, Jr., a proverbial "good guy with a gun" at a Hoover, Alabama, mall. *Slate* reported that other shoppers had guns drawn, but Bradford, a black man, "was the only person shot by police."[32] Reacting to the killing, Dr. Bernice A. King, daughter of Martin Luther King, Jr., tweeted, "While we're debating the forms of protest and people are maligning Kaepernick and saying he's 'disrespecting' soldiers, this young man, #EJBradford, who was in the U.S. Military, was a victim of what Kap was kneeling about." King concluded that "America must get right."

"Getting right" means seeing injustice for what it is and fighting it with courage and conviction. As author and athlete Etan Thomas wrote, "If you're not offended by the 22 veterans who commit suicide every day or the 2 million who don't have health insurance or the 50k+ homeless veterans but you're still mad at #Kaepernick & the #NFL players for taking a knee, you have greatly misplaced your patriotism."

FIVE

BATTLE FOR FAITH: UN-CHRISTIAN VALUES

I bless the Lord, he hath let me see which was
the clear ministry and which the wrong.
—Anne Hutchinson, 1637

Lehfed is a mountain village thirty-five miles north of the Lebanese capital, Beirut. It is a "site of sanctity, serene and calm, of vocation and prayer, with people who are firm and courageous believers, simple, generous, and with a firm faith in God and the Holy Virgin," poet Joseph Matar wrote. Brother Stephen Nehmé—a Lebanese monk who was beatified in 2010—was born and baptized in Lehfed. On his tribute page, the village's residents are said to "respect morals and values. They have a great faith and piety." Among Lehfed's places of worship is Our Lady church, one of the oldest Maronite churches in Lebanon. A modest rectangular stone structure overlooking a lush valley, it is where I was baptized, where my father was baptized, and where he was laid to rest next to his father and mother.

The Christian faith I grew up with in Lebanon—rooted in remote mountain villages, in old stone churches, in ancient cedar groves—is more than just ritual; it is community, it is history, it is spiritual practice, it is devotion and sacrifice. And importantly, it is a code of ethics. Religious values are similarly part of the fabric of American life. Pew's Dalia Fahmy wrote that the United States is "a robustly religious country and the most devout of all the rich Western democracies."[1] A 2017 Gallup poll found that approximately three-quarters of Americans identify with a Christian faith, roughly half of whom are Protestant, a quarter Catholic, and 2 percent Mormon. Among Protestants, a majority are Evangelicals. Another 6 percent of Americans belong to a non-Christian faith (Islam, Judaism, and others) while 21 percent "do not have a formal religious identity," according to Gallup.[2]

The separation of church and state is enshrined in the U.S. Constitution, and the words *Almighty, God, Jesus, Bible, Christ*, and *Christian* appear nowhere in the document that defines and binds Americans. But religion is at the heart of some of the country's most contentious political battles, and voting behavior is closely correlated with religious beliefs. More than half of Republicans—compared to a third of Democrats and Independents—are "highly religious." When former GOP congresswoman Michele Bachmann said in 2016, "This is the last election when we even have a chance to vote for somebody who will stand up for godly moral principles,"[3] she was reflecting the views of white Evangelicals who believe

America was founded as a Christian nation. These Christian nationalists are influenced by David Barton, a "prolific propagandist" according to the Southern Poverty Law Center, who has "long promoted the canard that our Founding Fathers never intended the separation of church and state but rather sought to construct a Christian nation."[4]

Was America founded as a Christian nation? Historian Mark Edwards posed the question to several scholars, including Steven K. Green, author of *Inventing a Christian America: The Myth of the Religious Founding.* Green responded that if the question is "whether the Founding Fathers relied on Protestant Christian principles in drafting the essential documents and in organizing the new governments, then the answer is a resounding 'no.'" Green continued, "If one refines the question to ask whether the Founding Fathers were motivated to act as they did based on their Christian faith, the answer becomes a little murkier, but the response is still 'no.'"[5]

Arguments for and against Christian nationalism boil down to dueling interpretations of the Founders' intent, but whatever the case, ideas of right and wrong, good and evil have always been part of America's identity. Moral imperatives are embedded in our founding documents. Things like "fairness and equality, freedom and courage, fulfillment in life, opportunity and community, cooperation and trust, honesty and openness," said linguist and philosopher George Lakoff, are "traditional American values and principles, what we are proudest of in this country."[6]

American exceptionalism—the idea of America's special character among nations—itself evokes moral superiority. Harvard University professor Stephen Walt noted that "over the last two centuries, prominent Americans have described the United States as an 'empire of liberty,' a 'shining city on a hill,' the 'last best hope of Earth,' the 'leader of the free world,' and the 'indispensable nation.'"⁷ The country's most admired public figures have spoken boldly of America's moral leadership in the world. In his inaugural address, John F. Kennedy said, "Let every nation know, whether it wishes us well or ill, that we shall pay any price, bear any burden, meet any hardship, support any friend, oppose any foe to assure the survival and the success of liberty."⁸

Our current partisan clashes over issues like immigration, health care, gun control, criminal justice reform, education, foreign policy, and reproductive rights are, at their core, moral disputes. Each party believes it speaks for America's conscience and each is unyielding in that belief. But only one regularly claims to have God on its side. The GOP is "explicitly selling itself as the Christian party," said *Atlanta Journal-Constitution* columnist Jay Bookman. In a May 2018 op-ed, Bookman wrote, "We get Lt. Gov. Casey Cagle, running for the GOP nomination for governor on the basis of 'defending our Christian values.' You get Geoff Duncan, in a Republican runoff for lieutenant governor, promising voters that he 'will never back down from defending our Christian values.' You get Jim Beck, the GOP candidate for insurance commissioner, prominently describing himself in TV ads as 'Christian. Conservative. Republican.'"[9]

But Christianity and morality are not synonymous, and invoking Christian faith is hardly sufficient to win a political debate. After all, religion has been twisted by tyrants to justify the most abhorrent acts. "The religious persecution of the ages has been done under what was claimed to be the command of God," Susan B. Anthony said at the end of the nineteenth century. "I distrust those people who know so well what God wants them to do to their fellows, because it always coincides with their own desires."[10] Extremists regularly cloak repugnant beliefs in moral arguments. As the United States Holocaust Memorial Museum's website states: "Wartime propagandists universally justify the use of military violence by portraying it as morally defensible and necessary . . . Throughout World War II, Nazi propagandists disguised military aggression aimed at territorial conquest as righteous and necessary acts of self-defense. They cast Germany as a victim or potential victim of foreign aggressors, as a peace-loving nation forced to take up arms to protect its populace or defend European civilization against Communism."[11]

The Republican Party has increasingly adopted extremist propaganda tactics, while using Christianity as a shield for policies that harm the poor, the sick, migrants, and children. The *Washington Post* reported that "government officials occasionally refer to the Bible as a line of argument—take, for instance, the Republicans who have quoted 2 Thessalonians ('if a man will not work, he shall not eat') to justify more stringent food stamps requirements."[12] Former attorney general Jeff Sessions sparked an outcry by using Scripture to rationalize the Trump administration's "zero tolerance" policy—the monstrous practice of ripping children away from their asylum-seeking parents and confining them in frigid holding cells. Human Rights Watch described the detention conditions for migrants and asylum seekers as "abusive," noting that the holding cells are commonly referred to by migrants and U.S. Customs and Border Protection agents as *hieleras* (freezers).[13] News anchor Maria Hinojosa, who has worked to raise awareness about these abominable practices, tweeted: "Hieleras. ICE boxes. And perreras. Dog cages. Words and things immigrants know well."

Attempting to justify the Trump administration's draconian immigration policies in a speech to law enforcement officers in Fort Wayne, Indiana, Sessions said, "I would cite you to the Apostle Paul and his clear and wise command in Romans 13, to obey the laws of the government because God has ordained the government for his purposes." Sessions went on, "Orderly and lawful processes are good in themselves. Consistent and fair application of the law is in itself a good and moral thing, and that protects the weak and protects the lawful." On Facebook, Ashton Pittman, a reporter and founder of the website Deep South Voice, wrote that Sessions "used Romans 13:1 to justify ripping small immigrant children from their parents and locking the children up in internment camps." Pittman noted that Romans 13:1 "was one of the key biblical passages that was used by Christians to justify American slavery." He asked, "Will America ever stop perverting biblical passages to justify its own cruelty?"

A number of religious leaders recoiled at Sessions's use of the Bible to defend an indefensible border policy. The Reverend James Martin, a Jesuit priest, said it was "obscene to use the Bible to justify sin. That passage in Saint Paul is about observing civic rule. All of Paul talks about how God's supersedes man's law. So to use that to justify ripping away kids from their parents and putting them in cages I thought was really appalling."[14] In June of 2018, more than six hundred members of the United Methodist Church filed a formal denominational complaint against Sessions for his role in the Trump administration's "zero tolerance" policy. *Christian Century*, a progressive ecumenical magazine, reported that the charges against Sessions included "child abuse, immorality, and racial discrimination," as well as "dissemination of doctrines contrary to the standards of doctrine of the United Methodist Church."[15] The charges were later dismissed "because the church can only govern personal conduct of its members, not political conduct," said district superintendent Rev. Debora Bishop, a United Methodist Church elder.[16]

NPR's Sarah McCammon, whose reporting covers the intersection of politics and religion, pointed out the inconsistencies in Sessions's Romans 13 reference: "That passage in particular if you read down just a little bit, it talks about obeying the law, but it goes on to say that the law is summed up in this, in love your neighbor as yourself. So this whole business of using the bible to support a political point of view is always a little fraught because the Bible is a complex book, and people have been disagreeing about what it really means for as long as it's been around."[17] Rosemary Agonito, author of *Hypocrisy, Inc.: How the Religious Right Fabricates Christian Values and Undermines Democracy*, expanded on McCammon's point that religion is often used to support contradictory political positions. "Jesus' followers, who all insist their values represent Christian truth, have advocated . . . for war and against war, for slavery and against slavery, for social justice and against social justice, for women's rights and against women's rights, for gay civil rights and against gay civil rights," Agonito wrote. "Nor is it unusual to find Christians affirming opposing values at the same time. The murderer of the abortion doctor argues that abortion is wrong because it constitutes murder. The Christian patriot justifies war that invariably kills innocent people, but argues that abortion can never be justified because it kills innocent children," Agonito noted.[18]

Republicans who cynically exploit Christianity to justify a border policy that amounts to state-sanctioned psychological torture make a mockery of faith. There is nothing Christian about the inhumane immigration policies crafted by Trump advisers like Stephen Miller, a sinister figure described by his own uncle as "numb" to human tragedy[19] and by progressive activist Jeff Tiedrich as a "dead-eyed white supremacist."

Forcibly breaching the bond between a parent and child—a policy later curtailed under intense pressure from digital activists—is an act of debasement and immorality. There is no valid legal, ethical, or religious case for it. It is the warping of Christian teachings to fit a nativist political agenda. As former paramedic Heather McMeekan tweeted, "There's no such thing as an 'anti-immigrant Christian.' Just in case you're confused."

Matthew Soerens, U.S. director of church mobilization for World Relief, wrote in *USA Today*, "when a government's response to a desperate mother who has fled threats of gang violence is seizing her children when she reaches our border in search of help and protection—even, reportedly, pulling a nursing infant from her mother's breast, or removing children under the pretense that the children are merely being taken for a bath—terror seems like an apt description. And the government is failing to serve its God-ordained role."[20]

When xenophobia becomes official government policy, the consequences are deadly. In December 2018, a seven-year-old migrant girl from Guatemala suffering from severe dehydration and exhaustion died after being taken into custody at the U.S. border. The ACLU released a statement calling for a thorough investigation, stating that her death "represents the worst possible outcome when people, including children, are held in inhumane conditions. Lack of accountability, and a culture of cruelty within CBP have exacerbated policies that lead to migrant deaths."[21] Filmmaker and activist Paola Mendoza tweeted, "Story is heartbreaking. I spoke to another family today that's been in custody since Tues. Her + her kids only given crackers to eat + hardly any water since detained. She's breastfeeding." When a second child died in immigration custody weeks later, college student Jacob Simpson tweeted, "The Trump Administration has successfully dehumanized immigrants to the point that this barely registers a thought to them. The callousness of this administration, its voters, and the Republican Party is astonishing. History will be damning to them, all."

The right-wing spin machine immediately went into damage-control mode for the GOP. "Dems, Progressives Quick to Politicize Death of Migrant Girl in Border Patrol Custody," asserted Fox News.[22] (This, from the media company that exploited the murders of Mollie Tibbetts and Seth Rich against their families' objections.) But no amount of obfuscation can change the fact that the GOP's approach to immigration treats migrants as less than human, in defiance of American values—and Christian teachings.

Joel Baden, professor of Hebrew Bible at Yale Divinity School, wrote in the *Washington Post* that "the Bible consistently spells out that it is the responsibility of the citizen to ensure that the immigrant, the stranger, the refugee, is respected, welcomed and cared for. It is what God wants us to do, but it also recognizes that we too were immigrants—and immigrants we remain." Baden argued that "no passage in either testament is as compelling or as clear on this subject as the vision of the final judgment in Matthew 25, in which Jesus will separate the righteous and the accursed based on how they treated him: for the righteous, 'I was a stranger, and you welcomed me'; for the accursed, 'I was a stranger and you did not welcome me.' When the judged ask when they ever treated Jesus in such a manner, he responds: 'Just as you did to the least of these, you did to me.'"[23]

Daniel Darling, author of *The Dignity Revolution: Reclaiming God's Rich Vision for Humanity*, cited Genesis 1:26 to state that "all human beings, including immigrants, were created in God's image." Darling wrote that "followers of Jesus should lead the conversation by recognizing the humanity of those who seek to enter our country and should reject language that assaults their dignity."[24] Rev. Dr. Chuck Currie, a United Church of Christ minister in Portland, Oregon, tweeted that a great nation "feeds the hungry, houses the homeless, provides health care for all, engages in diplomacy over war & bluster, welcomes immigrants, protects children from gun violence, and cares for the environment. How might God judge the USA when comparing our reality vs. aspirations?"

But appeals to conscience have done little to drive a wedge between Republicans and white Evangelicals, who are all too forgiving when it comes to the GOP's unscrupulous policies. In the 2018 midterms, Pew Research Center found that while Catholics split evenly, and other faiths and the religiously unaffiliated backed Democrats by a three-to-one margin, white Evangelicals broke seventy-five to twenty-two for Republicans.[25] Religious scholar Diana Butler Bass called the numbers "shameful." Dr. Tara Isabella Burton asked, "How did a religious group whose foundational sacred text explicitly mandates care for the poor, the sick, and the stranger become a reliable anti-refugee, anti-immigrant voting bloc?"[26] Robert P. Jones, author of *The End of White Christian America*, argued that "Fears about the present and a desire for a lost past, bound together with partisan attachments, ultimately overwhelmed values voters' convictions. Rather than standing on principle and letting the chips fall where they may, white Evangelicals fully embraced a consequentialist ethics that works backward from predetermined political ends, bending or even discarding core principles as needed to achieve a predetermined outcome."[27]

Shane Claiborne, an author and activist who leads a movement called Red Letter Christians, lamented that Christian apologetics once meant "defending Scripture and the tenets of our faith." Now, he argued, Trump apologists are "disgracing the name of Jesus." But on Facebook, Dale Mabry provided a sharp counterpoint, posting an earnest prayer for Trump:

> Lord save Donald Trump, that he might save us from socialism.

> Lord protect Donald Trump, that he might protect us from the Godless liberals.

> Lord strengthen Donald Trump, that [he] might fight to protect our precious babies from the abortionists.

Lord preserve Donald Trump's wisdom, that he might teach us how to glorify God.

Lord stay the hands of those who would harm Donald Trump, that [he] might stay the hands of those who come to take our guns.

Lord keep Donald Trump's strength, that he might protect us from violent invaders by building us a Wall.

. . . Amen.

"The theology of the 'Christian' right allows them to disregard Trump's moral failings," wrote Twitter user Drew Hoyt, a former Republican. Hoyt tweeted that "the 'covenant of grace' idea has degraded to the point that self-righteously declaring oneself a 'Christian' and denouncing 'godless liberals' is the only requirement for membership." David Smith, Washington bureau chief for the *Guardian*, spoke to attendees at the Values Voter Summit, an annual conference hosted by the Family Research Council. He wrote that their "consciences have found their own way of coming to terms with the seemingly glaring contradiction between their strict moral principles and Trump's private life, often by reaching for biblical terms such as forgiveness and redemption."[28] One attendee told Smith that Trump was "the people's president. He loves the country and he loves the American people who work hard and have been overlooked for years. The insiders in Washington forgot about us." Another attendee said that "God has chosen Donald Trump. He chose all of us to live our lives according to natural law."

In "God, Trump and the Meaning of Morality," the *Washington Post*'s Stephanie McCrummen wrote about members of an Evangelical congregation in the small town of Luverne, Alabama. An eighty-two-year-old woman said she feared "they are trying to frame" Trump. By "they," McCrummen explained, the woman meant "liberals and others she believed were not only trying to undermine Trump's agenda, but God's agenda for America, which she believed was engaged in a great spiritual contest between good and evil, God and Satan, the saved and the unsaved."[29]

"God always ends up raising up imperfect people like Trump because he is stubborn like a mule and tough like a lion," declared conspiracy-monger Alex Jones—who was sued for his unconscionable claim that the 2012 Sandy Hook Elementary School gun massacre was a hoax. In a video posted by Right Wing Watch, which monitors right-wing extremist rhetoric, Jones interviewed far-right pastor Rodney Howard-Browne, who claimed that "God gave America a last-minute reprieve with Trump."[30]

The seemingly unlimited capacity of white Evangelicals to excuse GOP wrongdoing was on full display during a 2017 special election to fill an Alabama Senate seat. Republican Roy Moore received 80 percent of the white Evangelical vote even *after* he was the subject of multiple accusations of sexual assault. While they countenance un-Christian policies that target vulnerable and oppressed people, white Evangelicals see *themselves* as an aggrieved group. Quoting Scripture to deter them from supporting Republicans is an exegetical exercise in futility—there are biblical interpretations to suit any political belief. And for the Christian right, those beliefs are most zealously expressed on a handful of social and cultural issues. Journalist Rose White narrowed them down to two: "This allegiance of Conservative Christians to the GOP . . . seems to come down to two issues: abortion and LGBTQ rights. These two issues have shifted and determined leadership races . . . They have divided a nation, and promoted intolerance."[31]

Both issues are major fronts in the Digital Civil War, and few right-wing political figures have been more engaged on the front lines of the fight than Mike Pence. "Pence is so notorious for his anti-LGBTQ stances that Donald Trump openly joked about Pence wanting to hang gay people," wrote Splinter News's Isha Aran.[32] "They don't call him the Hoosier Mortician for nothing," tweeted author M. Thayer Berlyn. "Straight out of the 19th century, waiting like a spider, deaf to everything, but his own eyes are alert." On 4chan, Pence was described as an "insane christian psychopath" and a guy who "eats babies and spits their bones out like bullets." Former White House aide Omarosa Manigault Newman said, "I'm Christian. I love Jesus, but [Pence] thinks Jesus tells him to say things. And I'm like, 'Jesus ain't say that.' He's scary."[33]

Twitter user "Resistadelphia" called on people to "Act Up! The homophobic VP and his 'Laying on Hands' religious extremist book club wants to destroy LGBTQ Equality. Falsely claims condoms and Sex Ed contributes to STD rates. Helped to deliver Evangelical votes for homophobic judges to favor repeal of Marriage Equality!" Digital strategist John Aravosis said that Pence is "so beholden to the religious right that even his own party finds him too anti-gay."[34] Progressive writer Susie Madrak tweeted, "Mike Pence is the same pious Pharisee who demanded prayer to stop Indiana's HIV outbreaks instead of clean needles."

Pence is "the most powerful Christian supremacist in U.S. history," wrote Jeremy Scahill at The Intercept, noting that "Trump is a Trojan horse for a cabal of vicious zealots who have long craved an extremist Christian theocracy, and Pence is one of its most prized warriors." Scahill argued that "Pence has been a reliable stalwart throughout his public life in the cause of Christian jihad—never wavering in his commitment to America-First militarism, the criminalizing of abortion, and utter hatred for gay people (unless they go into conversion therapy 'to change their sexual behavior,' which Pence has suggested the government pay for)."[35]

When Pence made an appearance at the Watchman on the Wall Conference and enjoined the audience to "share the good news of Jesus Christ," John Fea, a history professor at Pennsylvania's Messiah College, asked, "Just what did Pence mean by 'the good news of Jesus Christ?'" Fea suggested several interpretations: "Go ye into all the world and continue to teach people to live in fear rather than hope. Go ye into all the world and proclaim and peddle nostalgia for some of the darkest moments in American life. Go ye into all the world and proclaim the right not to bake cakes for people you don't like . . . Go ye into all the world and proclaim the need to call immigrants rapists and murderers. Go ye into all the world and proclaim and defend that guy who said that there were 'good people' on both sides in Charlottesville."[36]

Melissa McEwan, founder of the popular progressive feminist blog *Shakesville*, wrote about the "tension between Pence's claims of principled piety and his willingness to do anything to win. The way that Pence has bridged that irreconcilable conflict is to keep his ambition concealed; to be a snake who prefers the shadows rather than the sunshine." McEwan, who has written at length about Pence's record of bigotry as governor of Indiana, explained that Pence "will abandon all pretense of his much-lauded morality to align himself with a confessed serial sex abuser and white supremacist; he will invite and exploit hatred of marginalized people; he will change the rules; he will rig elections; and he will demonstrably lie about his knowledge of collusion with a foreign adversary that happened right under his nose as he ran the presidential transition."[37]

Pence is held up by Republicans—and a fair number of mainstream pundits—as a model of Christian virtue, but Democratic activists say he shares the propensity of the religious right to condone unethical policies and to support corrupt politicians. Polling supports that critique: an *Economist/ YouGov* poll found that "48% of Republicans say it's acceptable to vote for a presidential candidate who has done immoral acts, while only 19% of Democrats agree."[38] Jason Sattler, popular on Twitter as LOLGOP, wrote in *USA Today* that "American evangelicals, by and large, have decided that they can ignore Trump's personal morality because they are getting something far more important in return—the chance to impose their personal morality on others. And their role model for this devil's deal is the evangelical who made the Trump presidency possible: Mike Pence."[39]

In his book *The Family: The Secret Fundamentalism at the Heart of American Power*, Jeff Sharlet sought to explain the ethics of political expediency practiced by Christian fundamentalists like Pence. "There's always this idea: 'How can they tolerate this guy? He's a hypocrite,'" Sharlet wrote. "To which there's a ready response . . . 'And I'm a sinner.' That's in the vernacular. But there's also, especially in those elite evangelical circles, where you see guys like Christian right leader David Barton saying, 'Trump wasn't my first choice or my second choice, but I now realize that it seems that God has chosen him for this'—they don't see him as a godly man; they see him . . . as God's man, as the tool that God is using. And there's a long, long history of that."[40]

Journalist Michael D'Antonio, coauthor (with Peter Eisner) of *The Shadow President: The Truth About Mike Pence*, was asked by CNN's Christiane Amanpour if Pence was "on a mission from God, practicing what some evangelicals call Christian dominionism." D'Antonio replied, "Well, we already have an attorney general who quotes Romans from the Bible to justify his policies. Sarah Sanders said that the policy of separating children from their mothers at the border—these were asylum-seeking families—was very biblical. So, we're already in a realm where people are attaching scriptures to policy. And there is no doubt that Mike Pence is more devoted to this than Sessions or Sarah Sanders or anyone in the Cabinet is. This has been his main motivation throughout his life . . . to bring America along and make it a Christian nation."[41]

Christopher Stroop, a Stanford Ph.D. and "exvangelical" who launched the successful hashtag #EmptyThePews, explained that "traditionalist Christians literally believe that without absolute Truth and values derived from God, humans will become incapable of moral behavior, leading to social decline and disorder that can only be contained by authoritarian governance that will deprive individuals of their freedoms." Stroop made the case that "American democracy is up against a relatively large, well-heeled, and highly organized Christofascist bloc whose rhetoric reveals their contempt for pluralism and democratic norms and their desire to impose theocratic authoritarianism on the rest of us." He cautioned that accusations of hypocrisy are insufficient to deal with the problem, tweeting that "hypocrisy is part and parcel to any authoritarian system. Christian nationalism, like any nationalism, is intensely tribal . . . Evangelicals believe they have more of a claim to 'real American' status than non-Christians, non-whites, LGBTQ folx, etc.'[42]

Progressive activists see Christian fundamentalists like Pence not just as partisan foes but as a threat to democracy. Politics and culture writer Chauncey DeVega wrote in *Salon*, "Much has been written about Donald Trump and the Republican Party's authoritarian efforts to subvert and destroy American democracy, and their alliances with right-wing gangster capitalists such as the Koch brothers. But the enormous role played by evangelicals in Trump's victory—and in his enduring core of support—has not received as much attention from the mainstream news media." DeVega argued that white Evangelicals "have successfully completed a soft coup in America. This right-wing Christian movement is fundamentally anti-democratic. Their 'prayer warriors' do not believe that secular laws apply to them . . . Many evangelicals in the Christian nationalist or 'dominionist' wing of the movement want the United States to be a theocracy. In some ways, this subset of the evangelical population resembles an American-style Taliban or ISIS, restrained (so far) only by the Constitution.'[43]

That authoritarian streak is reflected in red America's support for the brute force tactics of U.S. Immigration and Customs Enforcement (ICE). In March of 2018, Sean McElwee, cofounder of Data for Progress, wrote an article for the *Nation* titled "It's Time to Abolish ICE." He argued that "the central assumption of ICE in 2018 is that any undocumented immigrant is inherently a threat. In that way, ICE's tactics are philosophically aligned with racist thinkers like Richard Spencer and the writers at the white-supremacist journal VDare." McElwee quoted Angel Padilla, the Indivisible Project's policy director, who said that ICE "is terrorizing American communities . . . They're going into schools, entering hospitals, conducting massive raids, and separating children from parents every day. We are funding those activities, and we need to use all the leverage we have to stop it."[44]

#AbolishICE has since become a rallying cry for progressive activists. "Keeping children in cages and denying them healthcare, deporting asylum seekers to their death after criminalizing them, ICE doesn't deserve our trust or our taxes! #AbolishICE," tweeted cultural organizer and activist Holly Roach. Reacting to a BuzzFeed News report about pregnant women being mistreated by ICE in immigration detention centers, "NativeKat" tweeted, "Where are the #ProLife people at? Where is the Catholic Church, or any Christians? I am #Curious why these babies don't matter to them. Where is the OUTRAGE?! #AbolishIce #NOW."

The inhumane immigration policies implemented by Trump and the GOP have exposed the moral decay of the Christian right. Tim Rymel, author of *Rethinking Everything: When Faith and Reality Don't Make Sense*, wrote that "the Christian right's agenda has been laid bare for all who choose to see it. They have abdicated any authority over the moral wellbeing of America in favor of obtaining political power and control."[45] As educator Laurence J. Peter (of the "Peter princi-ple") said, "Going to church doesn't make you a Christian any more than going to the garage makes you a car." Proclaiming Christian values doesn't make unethical behavior any less egregious. In fact, perverting religion to justify an immoral act makes the original offense even worse.

SIX

BATTLE FOR FREEDOM: A WOMAN'S CHOICE

I am not free while any woman is unfree, even
when her shackles are very different from my own.
And I am not free as long as one person of Color
remains chained. Nor is anyone of you.

—Audre Lorde

In September 2015, Amelia Bonow, Kimberly Morrison, and Lindy West collaborated to launch the popular hashtag #ShoutYourAbortion, which encouraged women to share their abortion stories. Like other successful digital campaigns, #ShoutYourAbortion quickly mobilized opposing sides of a raging fight. "Never going to stop shouting. There is no shame making my own decisions about my body and my life," tweeted web developer Ruby Sinreich. Lauren Barbato, a journalist specializing in reproductive rights and religion, wrote that her abortion was "funded by public money (MediCal). It saved my life. Funding for abortion is necessary." Sex educator Laci Green noted that "before abortion was legal, 5000+

women died every year," adding that "anti-choicers have no business calling themselves 'pro life.'" Writer Jasmine Sanders tweeted, "You can #shoutyourabortion or never tell a soul. But do remember that it's ALWAYS different for black women talking about their abortion."

"Abortion is normal; abortion is freedom; abortion is pro-life," tweeted *Bitch* magazine. Caroline Reilly, a writer for the publication, explained that "the hallmark of Shout Your Abortion has always been radical honesty, a perspective sometimes lacking in progressive circles that too often sees abortion as one of the most *difficult* decisions a woman can make." Reilly argued that such "transparency and frankness extends to not only stories of the procedure itself but the reality that abortion decisions are interwoven with other aspects of life: children, relationships, family, and sex."[1]

To anti-choice activists, the #ShoutYourAbortion hashtag was a moral affront. Theologian Seth Dunn warned, "Try to #shoutyourabortion on judgement day. Justice is coming. Repent and turn to Jesus." Ben Gill of the Christian Broadcasting Network (CBN) implored women, "Please don't #ShoutYourAbortion, there are thousands of couples waiting for a chance to adopt your baby. #ChooseLife, you won't regret it." The right-wing Blaze TV tweeted, "Let's go ahead and get this out of the way right now and set the internet on fire . . . Abortion is MURDER." Pro-Trump political analyst Scott Anthony complained, "Just when I thought the internets couldn't get any more mentally challenged, the alt-left pulls through and out does itself once again. #ShoutYourAbortion is likely the lowest low we will see for a while. That is, until alt-left pushes for #ProudPedo or #LoveACannibal."

A week after the campaign's launch, co-creator Amelia Bonow—who was forced into hiding after being doxxed and receiving death threats—told Jezebel's Madeleine Davies, "It is not breaking news that the anti-choice movement and conservatives in general rely on silence and shame to control and disempower women. SYA has just kicked the patriarchy in the dick. They are *so* angry with us and they can't figure out how to shut us up."[2]

The popularity of the #ShoutYourAbortion hashtag reflects the reality that a majority of Americans believe abortion should be legal in all or most circumstances. But public opinion hasn't stopped the most zealous anti-choicers from conducting a sustained assault on women's reproductive rights. A 2018 Pew Research Center survey found that only 15 percent of Americans want abortion illegal in all circumstances,[3] but with the far right holding sway over the GOP, and Christian fundamentalists like Mike Pence wielding their power in the service of right-wing extremism, a small minority of anti-choice activists are methodically chipping away at the rights of *all* women.

A preferred anti-choice strategy is the use of TRAP laws—Targeted Regulation of Abortion Providers. These regulations, which National Association for the Repeal of Abortion Laws (NARAL) president Ilyse Hogue characterized as a "sneak attack," are designed to impose undue burdens on abortion clinics.[4] In a piece titled "How Americans United for Life Has Been Pushing TRAP Laws Since Before Roe v. Wade," Bustle's Morgan Brinlee wrote that "there's one group you've likely never heard of that's been working behind the scenes to advance legislation restricting access to abortion for more than 45 years. Americans United for Life (AUL) calls itself 'the legal architect of the pro-life movement,' and it's been advocating for such measures on both the state and federal levels since before the Supreme Court handed down its landmark decision in Roe v. Wade."[5] Writing for the National Women's Health Network, Bridget Freihart pointed out that "AUL is the legal arm of the 'pro-life' movement with funding sources linked to the Koch Brothers." Freihart noted that "AUL's approach is to slowly chip away—one abortion-restricting law at a time—at the Constitutional protections affirmed by *Roe v. Wade*. This approach is known as 'incrementalism' and it's working."[6]

Rewire.News, a web-based publication that focuses on reproductive health, explained that "personhood" laws "seek to classify fertilized eggs, zygotes, embryos, and fetuses as 'persons,' and to grant them full legal protection under the U.S. Constitution, including the right to life from the moment of conception."[7] In "Women as Incubators: How US Law Dehumanizes Pregnant Women," health law specialist Linda C. Fentiman noted that an "alarming number of pregnant women have been criminally prosecuted for allegedly risking or causing harm to the fetus, based on conduct such as choosing not to deliver by caesarean section, having accidents, or attempting suicide." Fentiman argued that "statutes explicitly aimed at protecting fetal life have resulted in women's basic rights being held in abeyance throughout pregnancy."[8]

The ultimate target for anti-choicers is *Roe v. Wade*, the landmark 1973 Supreme Court decision affirming a woman's right to a safe, legal abortion. The Republican Party's successful effort to stack the Supreme Court with right-wing justices has placed *Roe* in jeopardy. "For too many women of my generation, a time before *Roe* feels like ancient history—but now, that history looms dangerously in the future," wrote Carmen Rios, *Ms.* magazine's digital editor.[9]

Legal and ethical questions about abortion—issues of life, conception, viability, fetal rights, and personhood—are the subject of extensive scholarship and debate. But in the final analysis, the abortion fight is about control. Whether one genuinely believes abortion is murder, or, as essayist Katha Pollitt wrote, a "common, even normal, event in the reproductive lives of women,"[10] the dispute over abortion invariably boils down to a woman's right to decide what happens *inside her body*, whether there are limits to her rights, and who determines those limits. Anti-choicers believe that the right to determine when life begins and to make private and highly personal choices about a woman's pregnancy is theirs, not hers. In short, the anti-choicers' mission entails quashing a pregnant woman's freedom, in order to satisfy *their* interpretation of highly complex and conflicting legal, medical, and moral issues. Ironically, this position is typically held by men who gripe about government overreach.

In the eighteenth and most of the nineteenth centuries, abortions "were allowed under common law and widely practiced," explained CNN's Jessica Ravitz.[11] The National Abortion Federation noted that "in the mid-to-late 1800s states began passing laws that made abortion illegal. The motivations for anti-abortion laws varied from state to state. One of the reasons included fears that the population would be dominated by the children of newly arriving immigrants, whose birth rates were higher than those of 'native' Anglo-Saxon women."[12] More recently, the GOP's embrace of right-wing extremism and Christian fundamentalism has contributed to the increased fervor of the anti-choice movement. As feminist and social activist bell hooks explained, "The idea that a woman's existence is only meant for bearing children is a central belief of both patriarchal and Christian societies. By demanding that women have access to abortion and contraception, feminism threatens this fundamentalist thinking."[13]

"If men got pregnant, abortion would be available free of charge and without restriction in every town and city on earth," wrote author Laurie Penny. "No man would be expected to justify his decision to terminate an unwanted pregnancy. It would be enough for him to say, 'I don't want to have this baby.'" Penny added that "if men got pregnant, they would not be forcibly penetrated with cameras and obliged to look at an ultrasound of the foetus before getting an abortion. Instead, sports channels and video games would be available in the procedure room, plus a free beer with every procedure."[14] Software engineer Isis Anchalee expressed a similar sentiment, tweeting, "I wonder how many more men would be pro-choice if they were forced to carry a football inside of them for 9 months?"

The paradox of the abortion battle is that while polls show that most Americans have nuanced views on abortion and choice, the strict anti-choice position is one of ethical absolutes, an unshakable belief that abortion at any stage kills an "unborn baby," that killing babies is wrong, and that abortion should therefore be forbidden. "What a parent may do to her child should not be up to debate. A child's death is ALWAYS tragic, and NO child should EVER die 'by choice.' Killing a defenseless baby, born or unborn, is a monstrous crime: against the child, against nature, and against nature's God. #AbortionIsEvil," tweeted anti-choicer Dave Burton. Jeanne Mancini, president of the anti-abortion organization March for Life, called abortion "the greatest human rights abuse of our time."[15] Anti-abortion activist Abby Johnson asserted on her website that "we're in the fight for life because we're pro-love. We see that every life, from the child in the womb, to the elderly—and in between, including the abortion clinic worker's life, have incredible value and worth . . . We believe that justice applies to every single human being on this earth."[16] Columnist Matthew Schmitz tweeted, "Since Roe v Wade was decided in 1973, American law has approved the killing of 60 million children. At present rates we kill 926,190 each year 2,537 each day 105 each hour These children have gone unnamed, unburied, unmourned."

Anti-choice groups employ clickbait headlines on social media to spread a "pro-life" message, sharing personal conversion stories, such as these, posted on Facebook:

Abortionist who performed over 1,200 abortions becomes pro-life.

What Caused This Pro-Abortion 'Femen' Leader's Pro-Life Conversion.

I had an abortion almost 30 years ago. I regret it to this day.

AMAZING: While pregnant, Suzanne was told by three different doctors to abort her preborn baby. She refused abortion every time and chose to give her child a chance at LIFE! Now, her daughter, Rachel, is 20! Watch this incredible story.

Anti-choicers have also exploited the rare circumstance of abortion later in pregnancy to influence public opinion. Political blogger Ed Kilgore wrote that anti-choicers use "lurid imagery and misinformation about the nature and frequency" of later abortions and that "their ultimate goal is to ban the vast number of abortions that occur earlier, mostly in the first trimester of pregnancy."[17] At Everyday Feminism, Laura Kacere explained that the term "partial birth abortion" was "created by the National Right to Life Committee, is not a medical term, and has been used primarily in political discourse, effectively perpetuating the misconceptions and stigma around late term abortions." Kacere noted that "due to either fetal anomalies or risks to the health of the patient, a pregnancy that is otherwise wanted/planned may be terminated," and that "people typically find out about birth defects around 20 weeks, and those faced with this possibility must make difficult decisions as they consider the quality of life for their family."[18]

In a Twitter thread directed at Mitch McConnell, Dr. Daniel Grossman, director of Advancing New Standards in Reproductive Health (ANSIRH), debunked the myths about second and third trimester abortions: "Hi @SenateMajLdr! I'm a board certified Ob/Gyn, clinical and public health researcher, and abortion provider. There are many reasons why patients need abortions after 20 weeks. Some due to the fetus having a lethal anomaly, some for the patient's own health, and others because financial and logistical barriers make accessing an abortion earlier very difficult." Grossman added: "One more thing—are you aware that many of the restrictions on abortion that you support are creating barriers to access, thus forcing patients to seek abortions in the second and third trimesters?"

In a fearmongering tweet, anti-abortion activist Devin Sena posted a photo of a pregnant woman with a sign saying IT'S MY DUE DATE TODAY. MY BABY'S HEALTHY. I'M HEALTHY. IN COLORADO, IT IS LEGAL FOR ME TO GET AN ABORTION TODAY. OUR LEGISLATURE HAS FAILED. But the claim was false—and the backlash was severe. "You are a lying sack of authoritarianism," replied author Thomas Levenson. "You know the claim is not true, and you use that lie to deny women agency over their bodies and the right to take action to preserve their own lives. People die because of people like you." Student and digital activist Sachi Shastri responded that "if you're blatantly spreading falsities just to further your 'cause' then your position didn't hold water in the first place."

The anti-choice movement's attack on reproductive rights entails a concerted effort to shut down abortion providers, among them Planned Parenthood, the leading provider of reproductive health services in the United States. Franklin Graham, a prominent evangelist and Trump apologist, wrote on Facebook that raising funds for Planned Parenthood "is like raising money to fund a Nazi death camp—like Auschwitz, except for innocent babies in their mother's wombs!" (Absent from Graham's inflammatory missive is that more than half of abortions conducted in the U.S. in 2014 were for Christian women, including 13 percent for women who identify as Evangelicals, according to research and policy organization the Guttmacher Institute.)

Comparing abortion providers to mass murderers, as

Graham did, is not unusual among Evangelical anti-choicers. In a *Marie Claire* piece titled "The Secret Evangelicals at Planned Parenthood," Laura Kasinof wrote that people on the religious right "have long been some of the loudest and most vitriolic critics of Planned Parenthood, an organization that provides reproductive health services to an estimated 2.5 million women and men in the United States each year. They've called Planned Parenthood a baby-killing factory and a bastion of evil."[19] Pennsylvania pastor Stephen Altrogge contemplated praying for the destruction of Planned Parenthood: "When am I supposed to pray God's destruction on someone else? ANSWER: When that someone else is KILLING babies."[20]

Biblical exhortations notwithstanding, there is no specific prohibition against abortion in the Bible. *None.* There are only tenuous extrapolations from verses that mention life, children, and pregnancy. Still, anti-choicers frequently invoke "Christian values" to convey moral authority. "I believe in the Bible," White House press secretary Sarah Huckabee Sanders told the *New Yorker*'s Paige Williams when asked about her views on abortion. "One of the things that makes Americans unique is that we value life. We think each life has intrinsic value and worth, whether you are a baby in the womb or an elderly woman," Sanders said.[21] But if Sanders and other Republican anti-choicers really believe each life has intrinsic value and worth, how do they explain a litany of GOP policies that devalue life? "If these people were actually pro-life, they would be fighting hard for healthcare, childcare, gun control, education and protecting the environment. But these anti-abortion people do not care about life, they just care about birth," said writer and comedian Michelle Wolf.[22]

The "pro-birth" critique of the anti-choice movement, frequently used by pro-choice advocates, holds that "pro-lifers" ignore—or exacerbate—threats to a child's life *after* birth. Alex Palombo, a communications specialist, explained in HuffPost that "legislators who are against women terminating their pregnancies are also the ones who want to cut funds to programs helping families. They aim to slash the budgets for SNAP, food assistance, child care credits, education, and health care."[23] Journalist and reproductive rights activist Asha Dahya tweeted that "saying 'abortion is murder' doesn't make you 'pro life' . . . It means you believe in the criminalization and shaming of pregnant people and legislation that forces them into the largest prison industrial complex on the planet." Digital media producer Ally Maynard asked, "If I'm a murderer for aborting a 5-week-old zygote then what do we call the people who enable mass shootings, let people die from lack of healthcare, pollute our environment, peddle oxycontin and shoot unarmed civilians?"

At CatholicVote.org, author and anti-choicer Eric Sammons acknowledged that "one of the most common criticisms of pro-lifers is that they only care about life before birth, and don't care what happens to a baby after she is born. Veteran pro-lifers have heard this canard for decades and typically shrug it off, knowing the reality of pro-lifers who work tirelessly at crisis pregnancy centers, soup kitchens, hospitals, and thousands of other outreaches." But Sammons conceded, "No matter the reason, by calling every issue a 'pro-life' issue, we dilute and fracture the brand. We make other, less important issues as important as the abortion issue."[24]

On 9GAG, a popular meme-sharing platform, a user posted an often-shared graphic about the slippery slope of the "pro-life" argument: "If abortion is murder, then blowjobs are cannibalism and masturbation is mass genocide." That may be a vulgar oversimplification of the debate, but the inconsistencies in the "pro-life" position are inescapable. Matthew Chapman, a game programmer and digital activist, posted a Twitter thread exploring the incongruity of the anti-choice stance, contemplating what should be done about "people who have two kidneys but refuse to donate one to a local hospital. Because if 'murder' includes causing the death of a being by denying it something from your own body that it needs to survive, that's murder too . . . Forcing a woman to carry a pregnancy regardless of her ability or desire is as irresponsible as forcing you to donate an organ regardless of your ability or desire."

In October 2017, science fiction writer Patrick S. Tomlinson sparked a heated debate with a thought experiment that challenged anti-choicers to answer a binary question. "Here it is," he tweeted. "You're in a fertility clinic. Why isn't important. The fire alarm goes off. You run for the exit. As you run down this hallway, you hear a child screaming from behind a door.

You throw open the door and find a five-year-old child crying for help. They're in one corner of the room. In the other corner, you spot a frozen container labeled '1000 Viable Human Embryos.' The smoke is rising. You start to choke. You know you can grab one or the other, but not both before you succumb to smoke inhalation and die, saving no one." Tomlinson stated that in ten years of posing the question to people who believe life begins at conception he had never received an honest answer: "They will never answer honestly, because we all instinctively understand the right answer is 'A.' A human child is worth more than a thousand embryos. Or ten thousand. Or a million. Because they are not the same, not morally, not ethically, not biologically."

Writer Madeleine Aggeler argued that Tomlinson's question "isn't a perfect parable, and it's a bit simplistic—notably absent from this scenario, for example, are the mothers whose health, independence, and physical sovereignty should be at the center of any abortion debate. It also ignores abortion's long, complicated history in the United States, one that is inextricably tied to issues of racial and gender oppression." She added that Tomlinson's thought experiment "is still valuable, though, because to be able to have real, productive conversations about delicate issues like abortion (as well as race, gender, economic inequality), we need to be able to [be] brutally honest—with each other, and with ourselves."[25]

Tomlinson spoke to *Salon's* Paul Rosenberg about the reaction to his tweets, telling Rosenberg, "A lot of folks online have been like, 'Oh that's just a modification of the trolley problem,' and yeah that's true. But it's also irrelevant."[26] The trolley problem—a thought experiment designed, among other things, to illustrate the moral conundrum of commission versus omission, of killing someone versus letting them die—is in fact highly relevant to the abortion fight. The *New York Times* noted that "the paradoxes suggested by the Trolley Problem and its variants have engaged not only moral philosophers but neuroscientists, economists and evolutionary psychologists. It also inspired a subdiscipline jokingly known as trolleyology."[27]

The trolley problem originated in philosopher Philippa Foot's 1967 essay, "The Problem of Abortion and the Doctrine of the Double Effect." As Berkeley law professor Eric Rakowski explained,

> She there imagined, by way of comparison, a group of spelunkers deciding whether to dynamite a companion stuck in the only exit from a flooding cave, a judge hanging an apparently blameless suspect to save more innocents from a bloody-minded mob, a pilot whose airplane is going down choosing to aim for a more or less populated area, a doctor who could kill a healthy individual to produce a serum or obtain body parts to save several patients from death, and, fatefully, the driver of a runaway tram whose vehicle will strike and kill five workmen unless he steers it onto another track where it will kill only one workman.[28]

A number of American philosophers have contributed to the trolley problem's modern variations, among them *Creation and Abortion: A Study in Moral and Legal Philosophy* author Frances Kamm, as well as her former colleague Peter Unger (one of my professors as a philosophy undergraduate at NYU). Kamm explained that the trolley problem "should not be understood so narrowly that the problem concerns only these two cases rather than all cases that are structurally similar."[29] And to Kamm's point, although thought experiments may never resolve the abortion fight, exploring their variations can be an enlightening process.

After Tomlinson posted his "save a child or a thousand embryos" challenge to anti-choicers, Berny Belvedere wrote a *Weekly Standard* piece titled "Here's an Honest Answer to That Dumb Twitter Rant on Abortion." Belvedere, who teaches philosophy at Florida International University, posited alternate versions of Tomlinson's scenario and argued that the reason we're inclined to save the five-year-old and not the embryos "is because our emotions, reactions, choices, are not always (and that is putting it generously) directed toward what philosophers and economists call the 'optimific' outcome." Belvedere admitted he would be inclined to save the child:

Why might I, personally, lead the child to safety in Tomlinson's scenario, rather than rescuing the thousand embryos? Because I would not be able to stare into the eyes of a child in perfect fear and pass him by. The embryos cannot do anything, in their present state, to match the terror and the dread of a child about to be engulfed by the flames. Let the thousand human lives haunt me afterwards; in this moment, they cannot haunt me more than seeing a helpless child be swept up in a fire. This does not nullify my belief that life begins at conception. What could be more human than for our actions to fail to live up to what we know is true and right?[30]

Right-wing author and podcaster Ben Shapiro made a similar point about the distinction between ideals and actions, writing that Tomlinson's argument "doesn't prove much beyond the fact that we make decisions all the time about the relative value of human life, often based on instinct. That doesn't make our instincts right; it doesn't justify non-hypothetical cases; it doesn't even prove Tomlinson's general point. But at least it allows Left-wingers to pour their instinctual scorn on conservatives without actually acknowledging the faultiness of their arguments." Shapiro proposed his own alternative to Tomlinson's question: "You can save the box of embryos or you can save the life of a woman who will die of cancer tomorrow. Which one do you save? If you choose the embryos, is the cancer-ridden woman therefore of no moral value?"[31]

Journalist Charlie Rae deconstructed Shapiro's argument, writing that "Shapiro makes hearty attempts at logic, I will give him that, but he pre-empts them by calling his opponents douches and calling their thoughts worthless. But I thought I would step in and offer not only a female perspective but a more rigorously logical one as well." Focusing on Shapiro's statement that "most pro-lifers freely admit the supreme value of already-born human life," Rae asked, "Why does Ben Shapiro refuse to prioritize the 'supreme value' of the women who get pregnant?" Concluding her point-by-point takedown of Shapiro's argument, Rae wrote, "All in all, I am glad that Shapiro put forth this rebuttal so publicly and self-assured, because now we can forever claim his own words in favor of woman and abortion access: he 'freely admit[s] the supreme value of already-born human life.'"[32]

In attempting to rebut Tomlinson, Shapiro and Belvedere argue that our instinctive response is not always the morally sound choice. Belvedere suggests that our visceral reaction to the prospect of seeing a child burn alive causes us to do the morally *wrong* thing and rescue the child. The flaw in this thinking can be demonstrated with another thought experiment. Instead of Tomlinson's frozen container labeled "1000 Viable Human Embryos," imagine one thousand preschoolers trapped in a locked auditorium at the end of a long hallway, and a single terrified five-year-old at the other end. You can't see or hear the thousand preschoolers (though you know they're in the auditorium), but you *can* see and hear the five-year-old screaming for your help. A fire is about to destroy the building and you have enough time to do just one of two things: race to the end of the hallway and save the five-year-old from certain incineration, or run to the other end and hit a switch that activates the auditorium's fire doors, saving a thousand preschoolers from a horrible death. If you hesitate, everyone dies.

Even though the children in the locked auditorium can't be seen or heard, how many people would save the one child and let the thousand preschoolers burn to death? The point is that our instinct to save a child over a thousand embryos can't simply be attributed to the fact that the child's pain is more "visible" to us. Our moral intuition tells us that saving one thousand children is better than saving one. Similarly, we feel that saving a five-year-old is better than saving one thousand embryos. That intuition matters, and to pretend it doesn't is to deny the importance of conscience and common sense.

The purpose of this exercise is not to get lost in semantics but to show the intractability of the legal, religious, political, and moral arguments on both sides of the abortion fight. "It all comes down to how you classify a fetus," wrote "Keithrb93" on Reddit. "If you don't believe it is murder, for whatever reason, then it seems reasonable to have an abortion. If you view it as murder, then of course it should be stopped or regulated heavily. The problem is the subjectivity of that classification." Subjectivity is precisely the issue. Writer Karissa Miller argued on Medium that "the moral implications of abortion are incredibly complex, drive to the core of what makes us human, and have constituted ongoing reflection and labored decisions on the part of women and men throughout human history." Miller added that "it is a private matter, that ought to be weighed gravely within the context of one's life and decided not by the interference of a government."[33]

Which brings us full circle to the problem of control. If there can be no consensus on the science and ethics, and if there are passionately held beliefs on either side, then *someone* has to have the right to make decisions about terminating a pregnancy—because abortions will be performed whether they are legal or not, and in the latter case, women will die. The pro-choice position is that the woman has the right to make decisions about her own pregnancy. The anti-choice view is that the government gets to make decisions for the woman. As political writer Amanda Marcotte explained "This is why feminists reject the 'pro-life' label and instead argue that conservatives are anti-choice. In cases where there's tension between 'life' and taking away a woman's autonomy, antis will pick the latter every time."

If anti-choicers want to go so far as to hand complete control of a woman's reproductive system to the government on the basis of the "sanctity of life," then taking health care away from the sick (as Republicans have attempted to do by torpedoing the Affordable Care Act) is a clear violation of their stated code of ethics, undercutting their anti-choice position. You can't selectively protect some innocent lives and not others while still claiming the moral high ground.

Registered nurse Alison Chandra tweeted about the GOP's

mission to repeal the ACA, writing that her son "was born with a laundry list of pre-existing conditions. Without the ACA no one would have to offer him health insurance. How is it pro-life to demand his birth and then make the life that follows it financially impossible?" Speaker and consultant Anastasia Somoza wrote on Medium, "Republicans have decided their goal is to destroy the ACA and enact massive cuts to Medicaid and Medicare, even though millions of people with disabilities rely on this life-saving health care nationwide, including many of the people whose interests they are supposed to be representing."[34] When GOP congressman Mike Johnson tweeted about "protecting the sanctity of human life," Twitter user "McBlondeLand" replied, "From the guy that voted to let my child die by taking away her health insurance. Fake pro life."

In January of 2018, the Daily Beast's congressional reporter Andrew Desiderio reported that "a bipartisan effort to stabilize the U.S. health-insurance markets collapsed . . . after anti-abortion groups appealed directly to Vice President Mike Pence at the 11th hour." According to Desiderio, "A group of pro-life activists met with Pence to lobby the Trump administration against supporting a health-insurance market-stabilization bill on the grounds that it does not contain sufficient language on abortion restrictions."[35] Claiming to protect "life" while jeopardizing the health care of the sick and poor is an untenable ethical position. But it is standard operating procedure for today's extremist Republican Party.

SEVEN

BATTLE FOR LIFE: BLOOD IN THE STREETS

This is the reality we face as young people in America today: the constant fear of being gunned down in the places we should feel the most secure.
—Emma González, Parkland shooting survivor

On the morning of December 14, 2012, a twenty-year-old white male shot and killed his mother in her Newtown, Connecticut, home, then drove her car to Sandy Hook Elementary School, where he gunned down twenty first graders and six adults. The sound of gunfire and screams could be heard over the school's intercom system. As first responders closed in, he took his own life. The weapon he used to slaughter the children was a Bushmaster model XM15-E2S rifle, an AR-15 variant. On YouTube, a reviewer marveled at "just how smooth of a shooter it is." A commenter replied, "She is a beauty."

In November 2014, Connecticut's Office of the Child Advocate released a report about the Sandy Hook massacre that opened with a tribute to the victims:

The authors of this report submit this work with acknowledgement of the 27 individuals murdered on December 14, 2012, and the terrible and incalculable loss suffered by all victims. Authors convey condolences for these losses and the grief that continues to be felt by the victims, families, and the community. We acknowledge and honor the lives of the twenty first graders who died at Sandy Hook Elementary School; they have been the sole reason for this report. Avielle. Ana. Allison. Benjamin. Caroline. Catherine. Charlotte. Chase. Daniel. Dylan. Emilie. Grace. Jack. Jesse. Josephine. Jessica. James. Madeleine. Noah. Olivia.

According to the report, the mass murderer shot his mother "four times with a Savage Arms .22 Bolt-Action Long Rifle. He then proceeded to Sandy Hook Elementary School, where he shot his way into the locked building. According to available reports, within 8 minutes the shooter had killed, with an AR-15, twenty children ages 6 & 7, and six school personnel: the school principal, psychologist, teachers, and teachers' assistants. As first responders were nearing the school, [he] shot himself with a Glock 20 10mm Auto handgun."[1]

The *New York Times* noted that the killer's mother was "a gun enthusiast, legally obtained and registered a large collection of weapons and would often take her sons to shooting ranges."[2] It was later revealed that he kept a spreadsheet of mass killings, which the *Hartford Courant* said contained "exactly 400 names, dates to 1786 and includes 17 categories." The spreadsheet was sorted by the number of dead. *Courant* reporter Dave Altimari noted that it was "remarkable for its attention to detail, with categories that included the weapons used, the number of dead or wounded, the date, time and place of the violence, and the fate of the perpetrator. Most of the incidents resulted in deaths. Most of the weapons were guns."[3]

Across America, gun violence has left a trail of carnage in schools, malls, newsrooms, clubs, bars, theaters, and places of worship: Tree of Life synagogue in Pittsburgh, Pennsylvania. Borderline Bar and Grill in Thousand Oaks, California. The Capital Gazette in Annapolis, Maryland. Santa Fe High School in Santa Fe, Texas. Route 91 Harvest music festival in Las Vegas, Nevada. First Baptist Church in Sutherland Springs, Texas. The list goes on. Nearly all of these gruesome mass shootings were committed by white males with a history of domestic violence—and with easy access to guns. The human toll of gun violence is staggering. According to the Brady Campaign to Prevent Gun Violence, in an average year, "17,207 American children and teens are shot in murders, assaults, suicides & suicide attempts, unintentional shootings, or by police intervention."[4] For all age groups, an average of 35,000 Americans die from gun violence every year, and nearly 90,000 are injured.

A study published in the *Journal of the American Medical Association (JAMA)* found that six countries—Brazil, the U.S., Mexico, Colombia, Venezuela, and Guatemala—accounted for half of the world's firearm deaths in 2016. These countries hold approximately 10 percent of the global population.[5] Gun ownership in America eclipses that of all other nations. Americans possess almost half of the world's civilian-owned guns, with estimates of the U.S. civilian stockpile ranging from 265 million to 393 million. The *Guardian* noted that in America "owning more than 40 guns is actually fairly common."[6] According to CNN, "Globally, the United States led the world in the rate of firearm deaths in youth among countries with available data in 2016. The rate in the US was 36.5 times higher than in a dozen comparable high-income countries around the world."[7]

America has a gun problem. But what that problem is depends on who you ask. For an overwhelming majority of Americans, the problem is too much violence and too much firepower in the hands of individuals who should not have access to firearms—let alone arsenals of deadly weapons. To address the problem, most Americans favor stricter gun control laws. An NPR/Ipsos poll found broad bipartisan support for measures including "requiring background checks for all gun buyers (94 percent), adding people with mental illnesses to the federal gun background check system (92 percent), raising the legal age to purchase guns from 18 to 21 (82 percent), banning bump stocks (81 percent), banning high-capacity ammunition magazines that hold more than 10 rounds (73 percent) and banning assault-style weapons (72 percent)."[8]

If you believe the NRA and its most devoted members, however, America's *real* gun problem is that gun rights are under assault, and that Democrats are scheming to confiscate all guns and repeal the Second Amendment. "Every issue that comes up, however reasonable the gun measure is, the NRA in D.C. and Virginia translates it as a message of con-fiscation to its base: 'They are coming for your guns,'" former Republican congressman David Jolly told *Newsweek*.[9] Right-wing media faithfully push the NRA line. Two weeks after the horrific mass shooting at Marjory Stoneman Douglas High School in Parkland, Florida, *National Review* posted an ominous-sounding Facebook video titled "Repeal the Second Amendment? 39 Percent of Democrats Say Yes." (The 39 per-cent figure was taken from an *Economist*/YouGov poll, which also found that 16 percent of Independents favored repeal, along with 8 percent of Republicans.) Facebook commenters weighed in:

> And here is the reason that these liberals need to be de-feated time n time again!! If liberals had their way none of us would own a gun except for criminals, terrorists and the almighty Gov't dictating whatever they think on us!!! —Albert Fierro

> I don't care if you're a Democrat or Republican white or black from f****** Mars I'm not giving up my right to defend my family to anyone, I for one will meet any attempt to disarm us my family with extreme preju-dice exercising My First Amendment rights agree or disagree I don't care. —Daniel Spurling

These are dangerous, un-American, and ignorant people that have to be stopped. Too bad it's not 240 years
ago—we could drag them out by their hair, and tar
and feather them for siding with the British. —Bob
Blomberg

You tell EVERY politician, Hollywood elite, million-
aire, billionaire to give up their armed employees and
then after NO protection for 1 year let's sit down and
talk. —Connie Hill

The Liberal outrage has nothing to do with these
deaths it has to do with power and control and you
cannot control a populace that can resist and defend
themselves, which is why they are so adamant about
gun control, gun registration and eventually confisca-
tion. If the issue is truly about people dying then those
that die at the hands of lone gunman are a rounding
error in the equation. But the Liberals learned a long
time ago how to exploit a tragedy and to never let one
go to waste. —John Albritton

What is notable about these rhetorical salvos is that on
guns, as with so many other issues, the right-wing position is
extreme and absolutist. This has far-reaching effects on public
policy. As reporter Natasha Lennard of The Intercept explained,
"all too often, when the bar for progressive legislation is set low

in the service of compromise with intransigent Republicans, tepid reform becomes the extent of the fight, not a pathway to more profound change."[10] This asymmetric polarization—the fact that Republicans, not Democrats, are becoming more extreme—affects everything from gun reform to health care to environmental policy. The far right, with the GOP's help, is pulling *everyone*, including Democrats, to the right with them. The result is that, instead of a healthy national dialogue about common-sense solutions to political and policy problems, Americans are forced to fight on the far right's turf.

On climate change, it is not *how* to solve the crisis, but whether it even exists. On health care, it is not how to guarantee a fundamental human right, but how to prevent the GOP from taking insurance away from sick people to fund tax cuts for billionaires. On economic policy, it is not how to ensure fairness and opportunity for working people, but how to stop the Republican Party from rigging the system for oligarchs. On immigration, it is not how to provide a refuge for migrants and asylum seekers, but whether we should kidnap and psychologically abuse children to teach "illegals" a lesson. On racial justice, it is not whether we should confront systemic racism, but whether athletes should be penalized for respectfully protesting during the national anthem. And on guns, it is not whether we should do everything in our power to protect innocent children, but whether we should be *arming teachers* and flooding the nation with more firearms.

Nearly eight in ten Americans want Congress to do more

about gun violence, but they are thwarted by the Republican leadership, which has repeatedly blocked effective legislation to deal with the crisis. For congressional Republicans, being at odds with public consensus matters less than appeasing their right-wing base and serving their NRA benefactors, who spent $54.4 million in 2016 to help elect Trump and secure GOP control of Congress. Illinois senator Tammy Duckworth wrote an impassioned appeal for common sense on guns, asking how "some politicians can consider the National Rifle Association's dollars more important than our kids' lives." Duckworth, an Iraq War veteran and Purple Heart recipient, wrote in the *Washington Post*, "I come from a long line of combat veterans who have taken up arms to defend this nation since before George Washington crossed the Delaware, and I spent decades in the military myself. So I understand why these kinds of weapons exist. But what I don't get is why semiautomatics that U.S. service members carry around Fallujah are being sold to teenagers at the corner gun store."[11]

In February 2018, journalist and author Michael Hiltzik penned a column titled "'Thoughts and prayers' and fistfuls of NRA money: Why America can't control guns" about the Parkland school massacre. Referring to Florida senator Marco Rubio, Hiltzik wrote, "We wonder if, when he's at home at night, he's comforted by the thought that he's one of the golden boys of the National Rifle Assn. Over his legislative career, Rubio has been the beneficiary of $3,303,355 in campaign spending by the NRA . . . Rubio knows who butters his bread." Hiltzik noted that Rubio's Fox News appearance the day after the Parkland shooting was "as close as one can get to the National Rifle Association's official line without issuing a press release on its letterhead."[12]

A week after the Parkland massacre, one of the survivors, Cameron Kasky, confronted Rubio at a CNN town hall. "This isn't about red and blue," Kasky began. "We can't boo people because they're Democrats and boo people because they're Republicans. Anyone who is willing to show change, no matter where they're from, anyone who is willing to start to make a difference is somebody we need on our side here." Kasky then asked a pointed question that brought the audience to its feet: "Senator Rubio, can you tell me right now that you will not accept a single donation from the NRA in the future?" Rubio tried to dodge, arguing that "people buy into my agenda. And I do support the Second Amendment. And I also support the right of you and everyone here to be able to go to school and be safe." But Kasky pressed him: "No more NRA money?" Rubio stammered, "But I—I—listen. I respect—you can ask that question, and I can tell you that I—people buy into my agenda. I will answer any questions you guys have about any policy issue."[13]

Columnist Richard Wolffe wrote that Rubio "did his very best impression of a sincere man who honestly wanted to keep children safe, if only there weren't so many complications to this whole lawmaking thing." Wolffe said Rubio "almost got away with it" until he met Kasky. "There were so many fine words of encouragement for all those feisty teenagers," Wolffe observed, "and so many regrets for the grieving families. It was a long-winded way of sending thoughts and prayers; the modern-day version of paying for tears at a Victorian funeral."[14]

But gun reform opponents were unimpressed with Kasky. On YouTube, a commenter named Dan Laroca wrote, "This kid last month was eating tide pods [a baseless claim] and now he's lecturing on what needs to be done about gun control . . . Everyone is responsible for his or her own actions, blame the one who committed this act and the cowards from the sheriffs office who were standing outside and were too chicken shit to go inside." To which a commenter named "Bleeding Eye Watcher" responded, "The NRA knowingly and willingly circumvents gun laws at the state and federal level. They've enabled the legal sale of military-grade firearms to criminals and domestic terrorists. By default, the NRA and everyone who supports them shares blame for every shooting in this country. Shooters don't obtain their weapons magically out of thin air." The NRA, of course, disputes that characterization, calling itself "America's longest-standing civil rights organization."

After the showdown with Rubio, Kasky—who had just survived a mass shooting—started receiving death threats on social media. He tweeted: "Temporarily got off Facebook because there's no character count so the death threats from the @NRA cultists are a bit more graphic than those on twitter. Will be back when I have the time for it." When Kasky and his Marjory Stoneman Douglas High School classmates launched the #NeverAgain movement to prevent gun violence, its members, including Emma González, were targeted by the far right. González told *60 Minutes*, "People have sent us a lot of death threats. And I, for one, am paranoid about a bomb being thrown in the window."[15] A letter sent to survivor David Hogg's home warned: "Keep f---ing with the NRA and you'll be DOA."

As NRA members harassed teens who had survived a mass shooting, a social media battle erupted between the gun-lobbying group and doctors who treat gun-violence victims, sparked by an NRA tweet that admonished "self-important anti-gun doctors to stay in their lane." Dr. Jennifer Gunter, an influential voice on social media, struck back: "Who do you think removes bullets from spines and repairs (or tries to) livers blasted by an AR-15? The tooth fairy? This literally is medicine's lane." Dr. Judy Melinek, a forensic pathologist, tweeted at the NRA, "Do you have any idea how many bullets I pull out of corpses weekly? This isn't just my lane. It's my fucking highway."

Right-wing hatemonger Ann Coulter jumped into the fray, telling Melinek that emergency-room doctors "pull cue balls, vines & gummy bears out of human orifices every week. That doesn't make them experts on pool, horticulture or chewy candy." Coulter was promptly rebuked by family physician Dr. Cathleen London, who tweeted, "We do examine assholes all day so it does make us an expert on them. You qualify." Emergency doctor Rick Pescatore tweeted at Coulter, "Hi,

Satan! I'm an ER doc. If you add up every gummy bear, cue ball, or copy of your shitty books Ive pulled out of orifices, it doesnt even approach the number of moms Ive had to tell their kids are dead from guns. Stick w/the xenophobia+racism youre so good at and GTFO our lane."

Dr. Esther Choo explained that doctors "are not anti-gun: we are anti-bullet holes in our patients." Trauma surgeon Joseph Sakran, who survived a bullet to the throat at the age of seventeen, tweeted, "As a Trauma Surgeon and survivor of #GunViolence I cannot believe the audacity of the @NRA to make such a divisive statement. We take care of these patients everyday. Where are you when I'm having to tell all those families their loved one has died." Sakran spoke to NPR about the heart-wrenching task of caring for the families of gun-violence victims. "When I walk out there to talk to these families," he said, "I often will just kind of stand there for a little bit and just look through the waiting glass window, and it's difficult. Sometimes I know that what I'm about to do is going to completely change your life. And I look at their faces and . . . these are all mothers, fathers, sisters, brothers that obviously care for this person who has just been injured. And so I try to be as empathetic as possible."[16]

But empathy is a foreign concept to today's Republican Party. "I don't think at the federal level there's much that we can do [about school massacres] other than appropriate funds," Mitch McConnell said, adding that it was a "darn shame."[17] The GOP's insensitivity toward gun-violence victims hasn't escaped the attention of digital activists. "Trump & the GOP have sold their soul to the NRA," wrote Twitter user Susan Covernton. Emmy-nominated writer Bess Kalb tweeted, "This is a pandemic that's killing children. And it's perpetrated by hypocrites who preach a doctrine of 'life' but take money from a profit-driven gun lobby."

For gun-reform opponents, the twenty-seven words of the Second Amendment—"A well regulated Militia, being necessary to the security of a free State, the right of the people to keep and bear Arms, shall not be infringed"—are inviolable. But from the perspective of activists seeking sensible solutions to the gun-violence epidemic, the Second Amendment has been misconstrued and misused by the GOP and NRA to block common-sense solutions. "The Second Amendment was never intended for someone who believes 'all Jews must die' to walk into a synagogue with an AR-15, shoot up a crowd of men, women, and children within minutes, and then open fire on police," wrote former Labor Department secretary Robert Reich. Fred Guttenberg, whose daughter was killed in the Parkland massacre, tweeted, "My daughter was amongst the nearly 40,000 killed by a gun last year. This is not OK and this is something we can do more about. We must continue to defeat the mentality that our desire to be safe is against the 2A. We must pass gun safety!!!!"

In a widely shared *New York Times* op-ed, retired Supreme Court justice John Paul Stevens summarized the history of the Second Amendment and called for its repeal. "For over 200 years after the adoption of the Second Amendment, it was uniformly understood as not placing any limit on either federal or state authority to enact gun control legislation," Stevens explained. "During the years when Warren Burger was our chief justice, from 1969 to 1986, no judge, federal or state, as far as I am aware, expressed any doubt as to the limited coverage of that amendment." Stevens noted that Burger "publicly characterized the N.R.A. as perpetrating 'one of the greatest pieces of fraud, I repeat the word fraud, on the American public by special interest groups that I have ever seen in my lifetime.'"[18]

But the NRA's influence on the Republican Party is a symptom of a larger problem in American politics, which is the self-reinforcing feedback loop between the far right, the GOP, and right-wing media. Far-right extremism is fueled and exacerbated by inflammatory right-wing media narratives, then embraced by the GOP, which in turn further radicalizes the right. This feedback loop has pushed U.S. politics further and further to the right and has transformed even the NRA itself. As Everytown for Gun Safety, the gun-control advocacy nonprofit, pointed out, "the NRA that was created after the Civil War to promote hunting, marksmanship, and safety training—and that supported common sense gun laws—no longer exists. Today's NRA would be unrecognizable to the founding members of the organization."[19]

The Republican Party's shift to the far right has created a political and social environment where human decency is trumped by fear, compassion by hate, logic by lies and deception. A party that boasts about its focus on "family values" and "protecting life" now shrugs at the slaughter of American schoolchildren—an indifference that shocks the conscience. Nelba Márquez-Greene, who lost her daughter in the Sandy Hook massacre, wrote that the GOP "functions like the NRA right now. Damage doesn't matter. They stand together no matter who gets hurt. Americans will die."

The GOP's callousness is reflected in all aspects of its policies. When Donald Trump and his right-wing media apologists fearmongered about a "migrant caravan" walking thousands of miles to the U.S. border, Vox's David Roberts argued that "inflating a bedraggled group of peripatetic refugees weeks from our border into a disease-ridden terrorist 'invasion,' an urgent, imminent 'national emergency' . . . amounts to a kind of willed delusion. It represents a collective agreement on the right to believe a narrative spun almost entirely out of whole cloth, draped over a reality to which it bears little resemblance."[20] That disconnect from truth, empathy, and compassion is a hallmark of the modern GOP.

Philippe Reines, an outspoken Democratic consultant, tweeted about the mind-set that has led to this Republican intransigence, arguing that Trump "is an extension of the Tea Party. Their goal was to blow up the government. Tear down policy after policy. There was no positive agenda. It was addition by subtraction. An agenda of destruction. Now it's a toxic mix of destruction & hate." To Reines's point, the GOP and its right-wing media operatives *have* become addicted to the energy of hate. Hate motivates people. Hate sells—hate directed at liberals, people of color, migrants, Muslims. When Fox News host Tucker Carlson asked unironically, "How'd we get to a place where it's normal that two parts of the country despise each other?" Shannon Watts, founder of the grassroots gun-safety powerhouse Moms Demand Action, replied, "I'm wondering if maybe—and I'm just spitballing here—it was the toxic network on which you host a show that advocates for white supremacy?"

EIGHT

BATTLE FOR POWER: OBSCENE MONEY

It is plain that we don't care about our poor people
except to exploit them as cheap labor and victimize them
through excessive rents and consumer prices.
—Coretta Scott King, 1968

Sheep Meadow is a fifteen-acre patch of calm in the heart of Manhattan's Central Park. Originally intended as a parade ground for military drills, it has been the site of numerous gatherings and protests over the decades. In 1968, the deadliest year of the Vietnam War, tens of thousands of demonstrators converged on the field for an antiwar rally. Civil rights leader Coretta Scott King—whose husband, Martin Luther King, Jr., had been assassinated less than a month earlier—spoke to the crowd about racism, poverty, and war. She opened her remarks by reading notes found in her husband's pockets on the day he died. "Perhaps they were his early thoughts for the message he was to give to you today," she said.

After reading her husband's Ten Commandments on

Vietnam, King delivered a speech that rings as true now as it did more than a half century ago. "There is no reason why a nation as rich as ours should be blighted by poverty, disease, and illiteracy," King said. "Our Congress passes laws which subsidize corporation farms, oil companies, airlines, and houses for suburbia. But when they turn their attention to the poor, they suddenly become concerned about balancing the budget and cut back on the funds for Head Start, Medicare, and mental health appropriations."[1]

Today, the skyline surrounding the field where King spoke is a stark reminder of the inequality and injustice she and her husband fought to end. Looking to the west, little has changed since 1968. Prewar landmarks line Central Park West: the Century, the Prasada, the Majestic, the San Remo. But at the park's southwest corner loom the gleaming brass-and-gold Trump International Hotel & Tower and, behind it, the twin-towered Time Warner Center, home to the five-star Mandarin Oriental hotel. To the south, there are the new sky-scraping giants of Billionaires' Row, which many Manhattan residents view as ego-stroking eyesores. Tech columnist Will Oremus tweeted that the super tall One57 (nicknamed the "Billionaire Building") was "a middle finger flipping off Central Park." On Instagram, Jim Thalman went further, calling it "a middle finger at the world."

Billionaire Michael Dell spent $100.5 million for a 10,923-square-foot duplex penthouse atop One57. Hedge-fund billionaire Ken Griffin reportedly plunked down $238 million for a 24,000 square foot penthouse at 220 Central Park South. A few blocks away, Commerce Department secretary Wilbur Ross bought a four-bedroom penthouse for $18 million from another billionaire, Andrew Farkas, then sold it in 2017 for $15.95 million. Curbed reported that Ross's lavish apartment features "hand-carved moldings, five wood-burning fireplaces, a huge living room with a barrel-vaulted ceiling, and a formal dining room that 'comfortably seats 30 guests.'"[2] Oil magnate John D. Rockefeller once said, "If your only goal is to become rich, you will never achieve it." But New York City's hedge-fund and investment-banking billionaires would beg to differ. Conspicuous consumption is a prerequisite for membership in a club where the price of a single-family condominium exceeds the combined annual salary of a thousand public-school teachers.

Bloomberg reporters Simone Foxman and Sonali Basak wrote that "America's last Gilded Age had its 'List of 400': the people said to be worthy enough, or at least rich enough, to climb the pinnacles of high society. Today, in an age of afflu-ence not even the Astors and Vanderbilts might have imagined, there is something closer to a List of 55. Its members are so rich that, in rarefied corners of Wall Street, they seem less like actual people than vast investment empires." Foxman and Basak reported that bankers compete to serve the hyperwealthy, "holding out investments that are tantalizingly off-limits to the rest of us, behind a velvet rope of bespoke investment banking. This is how the super-rich keep getting super-richer."[3]

Among those superrich is Wilbur Ross, whose $2 million loss on a Billionaires' Row penthouse barely made a dent in his net worth. Ross has been described by business associates as "obsessed with money and untethered to facts," according to Dan Alexander of *Forbes*. Alexander wrote that it is "difficult to imagine the possibility that a man like Ross, who *Forbes* estimates is worth some $700 million, might steal a few million from one of his business partners. Unless you have heard enough stories about Ross. Two former WL Ross colleagues remember the commerce secretary taking handfuls of Sweet'N Low packets from a nearby restaurant, so he didn't have to go out and buy some for himself."[4]

Ross, who owns a house near Trump's Mar-a-Lago estate and was a Trump adviser before being tapped as Commerce Secretary, epitomizes the profligacy and grift of the Republican Party. *Rolling Stone* described him as a "vulture capitalist with no experience in government, whose private-equity firm was fined by the Securities and Exchange Commission for bilking investors out of millions . . . a tidy fit for Donald Trump's Cabinet, which the president stocked with tycoons despite campaigning as a champion of the forgotten man."[5] Researcher Robert Maguire tweeted about Ross, "A theme of the Trump Era is that people who could have just followed ethics rules and stayed fantastically wealthy decided to risk criminal corruption violations to profit off of public office and . . . lost money. Maybe just don't be corrupt guys!"

Garish displays of wealth are a favorite pastime of

today's global mega-rich. In December 2018, days before news broke that a federal judge in Texas had struck down the ACA (Obamacare), jeopardizing the health coverage of millions of working Americans, a celebration was underway in India. Multibillionaire Mukesh Ambani had invited the world's political and business leaders to his daughter's wedding. Estimates placed the cost of the festivities at anywhere from $15 million to $100 million. *India Today* reported that "corporate leaders, including steel magnate Lakshmi Mittal, BP group chief executive Bob Dudley, 21st Century Fox CEO James Murdoch and Diageo CEO Ivan Menezes, among others, descended on Udaipur to attend the wedding festivities."[6] News18 said that the invitees included "Khalid Al-Falih, chairman of Saudi Aramco; Bill Winters, CEO, Standard Chartered Bank; WPP founder Martin Sorell; Kenneth Hitchner, chairman and chief executive officer of Goldman Sachs in Asia Pacific ex-Japan; Nicolas Aguzin, chairman and CEO, JP Morgan Asia Pacific; Farhan Faruqui, group executive international, ANZ; Klaus Schwab, founder and executive chairman of the World Economic Forum."[7]

"This is nothing but obscenity and decadence in a country where a large number of people are reeling under poverty," tweeted Ranjita Mohanty, author of *Democratizing Development: Struggles for Rights and Social Justice in India*. "#Ambani pays #Celebrities and #American politicians to dance at his daughters 100 million dollar wedding. Feeds a few poor in Rajasthan for publicity. Paid by starving people of #Andhra who dont receive dime from their #KGBASIN oil," wrote Twitter user "Meena," whose bio states, "Against Caste-Race-Gender-Oppression." Commenting on the famous attendees (who included Beyoncé, Arianna Huffington, Hillary Clinton, and John Kerry), Twitter user Ninad Dere joked, "Ambani is using beyonce, clintons, Bollywood like normal people use alexa!!"

The relationship of money to politics is one of the fiercest battlegrounds in the Digital Civil War. The fight is not just red versus blue (over Republican tax cuts for the rich and the enormous clout of right-wing billionaires like the Kochs, Mercers, and Adelsons) but the left versus the Democratic Party establishment (over campaign finance, student debt, the failures of capitalism, resurgent socialism, and the roots of economic inequality).

Concerns over income and wealth disparities in the United States are hardly new. As early as the 1600s, English explorer Captain John Smith wrote in his *Generall Historie of Virginia* that "this deare bought Land with so much bloud and cost, hath onely made some few rich, and all the rest losers."[8] Three centuries later, the Gilded Age saw "exploding economic inequality, stagnant living standards, growing concern about monopolies, devastating financial crises, multiple 'wave' elections in which control of Congress suddenly shifted, two presidential elections in which the popular-vote winner came up short in the Electoral College, brazen political corruption, frequent pronouncements that the American republic was doomed, and seemingly unending turmoil over race and national identity," wrote *Bloomberg* columnist Justin Fox, drawing obvious parallels with the modern era.[9]

Income inequality loomed large over the 2016 presidential primary between Bernie Sanders and Hillary Clinton. Sanders repeatedly railed against "millionaires and billionaires" and accused Clinton of being in the pocket of Wall Street donors. She was attacked by left and right for her paid speeches to big banks, and later conceded the bad "optics" of those speeches. The reverberations from the 2016 race have had a lingering effect on Democratic politics, provoking ferocious social media battles between Clinton and Sanders supporters that have spilled over into the 2020 presidential primary.

Glenn Greenwald, a lawyer and cofounding editor of The Intercept, articulated the left's position: "The inability of rich neoliberal centrist elites in western capitals to understand— or even hide their scorn for—the anger & grievances of rural and working-class people over their economic suffering is one of the 2 or 3 most important causes of contemporary political changes." In *The Chapo Guide to Revolution: A Manifesto Against Logic, Facts, and Reason*, Chapo Trap House, a political satire collective, wrote, "The mummies in the Democratic party are busy trying to rebrand Clintonesque bromides like 'entrepreneurship' and 'education reform,' while the average, young working person is desperate for health care, free college, and a steady job that pays them in something other than Applebee's Lunch Combo coupons." The Chapo authors continued, "Our case is simple: capitalism, and the politics it spawns, is not working for anyone under 30 who is not a sociopath. It's not supposed to. The actual lived experience of the free market feels distinctly un-free."[10]

But Clinton backers have questioned the motives and tactics of Sanders's supporters. Writer Kara Calavera tweeted that "Bernie created a toxic culture of brocialism and stood back while his army of triggered dudebros 'Well, actually'ed me at best, and harassed and threatened me at worst. The fact that I won't give him a second chance says that I'm a strong woman who won't take abuse from men." Marcus H. Johnson, who writes about how race affects policy and governance, tweeted, "Alt-left: 1. Anti-identity politics 2. Claims to be socialist but pro any dictator abroad who is anti-US regardless of economics 3. Conspiracy theorists 4. Wanted Trump over Clinton 5. Believes alt right can be worked with to defeat 'global elites.'"

The tension between Clinton and Sanders supporters reflects a wider dispute between leftists and Democrats over issues of intersectionality, "identity politics," and economic justice. South Asian queer activist Monjula Ray tweeted that "Bernie Sanders courts a lot of people who anger the base of the democratic party. He talks in a way that alienates much of the base too . . . as someone who is very representative of the Democratic base, and is not a moderate voter really, they lie about why we don't support Bernie. To begin with, I don't support people who center white men. I don't support people who deride civil rights as identity politics." Social media manager Bianca Delarosa tweeted, "I hate Bernie's racial ignorance and his insistence on class reductionism." Delarosa argued emphatically that until Sanders "provides a mechanism for bridging the Gap between white men and black women I am a HARD PASS." "Ragnarok Lobster" wrote, "I tweet for the people who are accused of weaponizing identity politics every time they point out Bernie Sanders is only interested in helping the so-called white working class."

Briahna Joy Gray, an attorney and columnist, provided a counterpoint, tweeting, "I said it before and I'll say it again: Bernie Sanders doesn't have a black problem. He has a pundit problem." James J. Zogby, founder and president of the Arab American Institute (AAI), wrote, "This is what I love about #Bernie. He's principled and direct and he's unwilling to accept any form of economic, racial, and social injustice. And he's angry enough to want to fight to make it right." CauseWired founder Tom Watson disagreed, writing of Sanders: "I oppose him politically, particularly in the context of his separatist movement aimed at chopping up [the] Democratic Party." Watson added that the Vermont senator's "theory of change is rubbish."

But for many on the left, Sanders is a symbol of opposition to the status quo, an indictment of a Democratic Party that has failed to effectively counter Republican extremism. Activist Nomiki Konst tweeted that Sanders "challenged capitalism," and that it is "strategically foolish for Democrats [to] resist his ideas." Kyle Kulinski, host of the YouTube channel Secular Talk, tweeted that "Bernie is clearly dedicated to the canon of social democratic policies we all want." *New York*

Magazine's Jonathan Chait argued that "Sanders attracts the intense support of a small left-wing intellectual vanguard who see American politics in fundamentally different terms than most Democrats do. The primary struggle in American politics as they see it is not between liberalism and conservatism, but between socialism and capitalism . . . The struggle between Sanders and other Democrats strikes them as far more significant than the contest between the non-socialist Democrats and the Republicans."[11]

As the ideological fight rages online between Democrats and leftists, another front in the Digital Civil War involves the Republican Party's "reverse Robin Hood" policies—stealing from working people to help the 1 percent. During the 2017 debate over the proposed Republican tax plan (dubbed the #taxscam on social media), "lark," a member of the online forum Democratic Underground, commented that the debate wasn't really about the economy, but about "taking available money and moving it all to the rich from the pockets of the middle class and poor . . . they are stealing our Medicare and Medicaid to stash in their banks, buy more elections and turn us permanently into an oligarchy." Political strategist Karine Jean-Pierre tweeted that the GOP tax plan was a "wealth grab that takes from the poor and gives to the rich. Oh, and takes healthcare away from millions."

On Twitter, Trump supporters fired back. A user named "HARLEY" hailed Trump's record: "The Stock Market King. The Job King. The Economy King. The MAGA King. The

Trigger Of Libs . . . The People's voice . . . The Patriots Choice for President . . . The Man." Another user named Bradley Scott tweeted, "Thanks @POTUS for: -tax cuts -a growing economy -progress with North Korea -judicial appointments -your tweets . . . Comey, McCabe, Stormy, Mueller, #FakeNews, Libs & all those working against you can all go screw themselves!"

Right-wing rhetorical fireworks aside, there is abundant data demonstrating that Republican policies disproportionately benefit the rich. Economist and policy adviser Robert J. Shapiro wrote in December 2017 that "over the last 40 years, income inequality has accelerated when Republicans held the White House, the Congress or both, and slowed when Democrats were in charge." Shapiro pointed out that in the four-decade span from 1977 and 2014, "when Republicans held the presidency, the top one percent's rising share of all post-tax income accelerated on average by 0.4 percentage-points, while under Democratic presidents their rise correspondingly slowed by 0.4 percentage points." He concluded, "Helping the rich and letting those in the bottom half fend for themselves, it seems, is now part of the modern GOP's DNA."[12]

But Republican politicians are deeply invested in their faux-populist image, posing as working-class champions and contrasting themselves with "elites" in academia, Hollywood, and Washington. The *Washington Post*'s Eugene Scott wrote that "few things unite conservatives more than expressing a deep disdain for 'the elites'—a vague term with no clear definition beyond 'them.'"[13] Nobel Prize–winning economist

Paul Krugman put the lie to the GOP's anti-elitist con, arguing that "when it comes to policies that affect workers, Trump
has created a team of cronies: Almost every important position has gone to a lobbyist or someone with strong financial
connections to industry. Labor interests have received no
representation at all."[14] Twitter user Sarah Kerrigan argued
that "all of that 'elites' rhetoric during the election was cover/
distraction for a band of criminal oligarchs and their expanding #kleptocracy."

The GOP's performative populism descended into
self-parody when Matt Schlapp, lobbyist and chairman of
the American Conservative Union, tweeted that he and his
wife walked out of the White House correspondents' dinner because they'd had enough of "elites mocking all of us."
The tweet garnered more than twenty thousand comments,
the majority of which mocked Schlapp for the fact that he *is* the
D.C. elite, and that he tweeted "from a limousine en route to an
exclusive after-party organized by NBC/MSNBC," as the *New
York Times* reported.[15] "Only in conservative America could the
chair of a multi million dollar lobbying firm claim that, of the
two of them, a stand up comedian is the 'elite' member of society who wields power and influence," observed Twitter user
Gavin Greenwalt.

Republican politicians may genuflect to working
Americans, but their economic policies are designed to reward
the well heeled and well connected. Behavioral scientist
Caroline Orr tweeted that the GOP "is happy to increase [the]

deficit if it means tax cuts for the rich, but not if it means help-ing everyday Americans." While GOP leaders claimed their much-touted Tax Cuts and Jobs Act of 2017 would pay for itself, Business Insider reported that "their overhaul of the tax code isn't producing the desired result."[16] Vox's Emily Stewart noted that when Republicans passed their tax cut "they said it would come with a big wage boost for American workers. Except it hasn't."[17] In fact, an analysis by the Institute on Taxation and Economic Policy (ITEP) and Prosperity Now, a nonprofit that advocates on behalf of working families, found that "more than 40% of all tax cuts from the Tax Cuts and Jobs Act go to the White households in the top 5% of earners (with incomes of $243,000 or more), despite only representing 3.9% of all tax returns."[18] At *The American Prospect*, Manuel Madrid noted, "Under the new tax law, wealth is valued even more highly than work than it was before—and racial gaps in wealth are even larger than racial gaps in income."[19]

Pat Garofalo, managing editor of TalkPoverty, refuted the talking point that bonus pay increased under the Republican tax bill. "Any bonus pay for workers is obviously good, but don't buy that there were widespread bonuses because of the GOP tax bill," Garofalo wrote, "bonus compensation is only up 2 cents per hour since the bill passed." At the *Nation*, Joshua Holland explained that the Republican tax bill "finances over $1 trillion in cuts skewed overwhelmingly toward corporations and the wealthy through deficit spending." Holland argued that "it's the brazenness with which the Republican Party abandoned any last remaining pretense of caring about deficits or federal spending that may come back to haunt them, and mark a shift in the political landscape around taxes and spending."[20]

On Twitter, business owner Renee Hoagenson wrote that the "#GOP #TaxScam isn't working. It didn't work for Reagan, Bush I or II . . . 1) Wages haven't kept up w/ inflation. 2) The stock market is down. 3) The deficit is on track to surpass $1 trillion." Resistance activist Helen Doan drew a connection between the Republican tax bill and Trump's obsession with a wall along the Mexico border: "U could've applied some of this year's $200+ Billion giveaway via ur #TaxScam for the RICH to your stupid wall." Historian Heather Cox Richardson provided valuable context on the tax debate, noting that for the GOP "tax cuts to destroy the New Deal state became a political law . . . even though folks like government programs. Leaders convinced voters that gov't programs gave tax dollars from hardworking white men to lazy POC and women."

To highlight the Republican Party's skewed budget priorities, Democrats on the Senate Budget Committee listed a series of programs that could have been funded with the GOP's nearly $1 trillion on military spending and tax breaks for the rich and large corporations:

- Very nearly eliminate poverty for all Americans of any age. Estimated cost: $174 billion.
- Pay the one-year average of the 10-year infra-

structure funding gap. Estimated cost: $144 billion.

- Provide high-quality early care and education (ECE) for children from birth to kindergarten. Estimated cost: $140 billion.

- Eliminate child poverty by simply boosting the income of all families with children (and children who do not live with their families) over the poverty line. Estimated cost: $69 billion.

- Double the budget of the National Science Foundation, the National Institutes of Health, the Centers for Disease Control and Prevention, the National Oceanic and Atmospheric Administration and the United States Geologic Survey. Estimated cost: $61 billion.

- Make public colleges and universities tuition-free for working families, cut student loan interest rates in half, and allow every American with student debt to refinance at the lowest interest rate possible. Estimated cost: $60 billion.

- Double the $1.40 per-meal allowance in the Supplemental Nutrition Assistance Program. Estimated cost: $70 billion.

- End homelessness in America. Estimated cost: $22.5 billion.[21]

Yet, given the option to fund programs that could end homelessness, cut student-loan rates, eliminate child poverty, provide early childhood care, and invest in infrastructure, Republicans have repeatedly chosen to enrich billionaires.

The GOP's role as a vehicle for the right-wing billionaire class to consolidate wealth and power is the subject of Nancy MacLean's illuminating book *Democracy in Chains: The Deep History of the Radical Right's Stealth Plan for America*. MacLean wrote that the "single most powerful and least understood threat to democracy today" is "the attempt by the billionaire-backed radical right to undo democratic governance." MacLean argued that "it wasn't until the early 2010s that the rest of us began to sense that something extraordinarily troubling had somehow entered American politics. All anyone was really sure of was that every so often, but with growing frequency and in far-flung locations, an action would be taken by governmental figures on the radical right that went well beyond typical party politics, beyond even the extreme partisanship that has marked the United States over the past few decades." MacLean asked, "What if the goal of all these actions was to destroy our institutions, or at least change them so radically that they became shadows of their former selves?"[22]

Veteran journalist Bill Moyers sounded a similar alarm at the Brennan Center's 2013 Legacy Awards Dinner, arguing that the far right "is now nourished by streams of 'dark money' unleashed by the gift bestowed on the rich by Citizens United." Moyers said that "we don't have emperors yet, but we do have the Roberts Court that consistently privileges the donor class . . . No emperors yet, but one of our two major parties is now dominated by radicals engaged in a crusade of voter suppression aimed at the elderly, the young, minorities and the poor while the other party, once the champion of everyday working people, has been so enfeebled by its own collabora- tion with the donor class that it offers only token resistance to the forces that have demoralized everyday Americans."[23] Progressive political commentator Mike Figueredo echoed Moyers's argument, writing that "the American political pro- cess has been corrupted and commodified, and democracy has been hollowed out by capitalism." Figueredo argued that "the lawmakers with the power needed to address this have effec- tively become tools for special interests, and as they sit idly by, income inequality gets worse. As each year passes, Americans become increasingly desperate, and this is not only harmful for the well-being of Americans at the individual-level, but it's destabilizing at a national-level."

The Republican Party's allegiance to the oligarchy comes at a steep cost. As journalist Eric Levitz explained, "A tiny elite is binge-eating the global economic pie while 7 billion humans fight for their table scraps."[24] Axios noted that "the 7 million richest people in the world (the top 0.1%) have taken home 13.8% of all economic growth since 1980, according to the 2018 World Inequality Report from the Paris School of Economics. That's as much as the poorest half of the world, or 3.8 billion people."[25] Democratic senator and presidential candidate

Kamala Harris tweeted, "The gap between the rich and the poor continues to grow. Tackling income inequality is one of the most pressing issues of our time. It must be addressed through living wages, equal pay for equal work, and access to quality, affordable education." Columnist Michelle Goldberg noted the irony that "people with thousands of dollars in debt are shamed, while those with millions of dollars in debt rule the world."[26] Or, as industrialist J. Paul Getty put it, "If you owe the bank $100, that's your problem. If you owe the bank $100 million, that's the bank's problem."

Extreme inequality is extreme injustice. Actor Anton Blake wrote that the "lacuna between the Haves, the Have-Nots—and the Have-Yachts couldn't be wider. How can this insanity—this glaring inequality on such a gigantic scale—be sustainable, one wonders?" It isn't sustainable, not without immense human suffering. *Forbes*'s thirty-second annual ranking of the world's billionaires identified a record 2,208 billionaires with a combined net worth of $9.1 trillion, enough wealth to eradicate or ameliorate the plagues of poverty, disease, homelessness, and hunger. As Oxfam tweeted, "26 billionaires now own as much as 3.8 billion people." It is a moral travesty that a tiny fraction of the global population hoards such a staggering proportion of the world's wealth and resources. "No one should be a billionaire," tweeted author and activist Feminista Jones. Indeed, no individual should be worth a *billion dollars* when children are starving.

NINE

BATTLE FOR TOMORROW: THE CLIMATE WARRIORS

They claim this mother of ours, the earth, for their
own, and fence their neighbors away; they deface her
with their buildings and their refuse.
—Tatanka-Iyotanka (Sitting Bull), 1877

The steady stream of political spin, disinformation, and propaganda put forth by the Republican Party and right-wing media has created a reality gap between red and blue Americans. That chasm between blue facts and red myths has become the defining feature of modern U.S. politics and a major contributor to the Digital Civil War. It manifests across a range of issues, most saliently in the fight over climate change, an issue that brings the Republican Party's extremism into sharp focus.

The denial of human-induced climate change flies in the face of scientific consensus, common sense, and the natural instinct for self-preservation. It also runs afoul of virtually every principle Republicans claim to hold dear. Climate deniers who proclaim to uphold family values support policies that endanger *all* families. Those who say they abide by Christian ethics ignore Bible verses about being good stewards of God's creation. Those who enjoy farming, hunting, fishing, and camping show their contempt for the natural world that sustains them. Those who vehemently oppose a woman's choice on the basis of the "sanctity of life" jeopardize the health and life of future generations. Those who claim to "support the troops" disregard unequivocal statements by the U.S. military that climate change is real, is caused by humans, and is already resulting in substantial harm.

The red-blue fight over climate denial has taken on renewed urgency with the publication of a spate of new studies painting a harrowing picture of the consequences of global climate change. Environmental activist Mike Hudema captured the gravity of the crisis in a single tweet: "Dear Humanity, Climate change threatens our existence. If we don't act soon there'll be catastrophic biodiversity loss and untold amounts of human misery. Time is running out.—Yours, 15,000 concerned scientists." Climate scientist Kate Marvel told *Meet the Press*: "We are talking about something that affects the planet that we live on . . . It should feel overwhelming, because it is overwhelming."

But the Republican Party is determined to deny incontrovertible facts about climate change, blocking the urgent action necessary to deal with the crisis. In November 2018, climate expert Dr. J. Marshall Shepherd wrote for *Forbes* about the *Fourth National Climate Assessment*, a report compiled by thirteen federal agencies and more than three hundred climate scientists that warned of ocean acidification, waterborne illnesses, declining crop production, and deadly heat waves as a result of climate change. Shepherd pointed out that the Trump administration tried to bury the report by releasing it during a holiday: "The day after Thanksgiving is college football downtime for many of us and Black Friday shopping for others. I suspect it is certainly not considered a 'textbook' date . . . for releasing something important and newsworthy. The Trump Administration released the 4th National Climate Assessment report on that day." But as Shepherd noted, "That tactic may have backfired. Movements like the #ClimateFriday hashtag sprouted on social media to get the word out, and the media covered the report vigorously."[1]

A growing number of influential climate scientists have used social media to educate the public about climate change, among them Katharine Hayhoe, who tweeted that there are "five stages to climate denial: 1/ it's not real (it's a Chinese hoax) 2/ it's not humans: let's witch-hunt the scientists 3/ warmer is better! 4/ it's too expensive to fix 5/ it's too late; you scientists really should have warned us earlier." Trump and his fellow Republican climate deniers have gone through each of those stages. Asked about the *Fourth National Climate Assessment*, Trump had a four-word response: "I don't believe it." Breitbart News amplified Trump's denial, with writer Penny Starr arguing that the report "has gained praise from leftists and left-wing environmental groups as a dire warning of the coming death and destruction in the United States if we don't stop global warming. But critics of the report, including scientists, have slammed it as 'exaggeration,' bad science and even said its conclusions are 'false.'"[2] Breitbart News commenters agreed:

> Democrats who believe the Climate hoax think killing babies is the CURE for planet earth. I kid you not, they're that demented. —"Ratburt Deplorable"

> I am too worried about the drastic climate change of illegal Invaders entering our country. Stop the fallout from our poisoning propaganda media who has polluted the tiny brains of millions of libtards. Build the Wall Stop them All. MSM induced TDS [Trump Derangement Syndrome] is the Libtard Downfall. —"Trump Train aka Honey Badger"

> I'm a firm believer in climate change: Spring Summer Autumn Winter.—"Dark Knight"

But *denying* reality doesn't *alter* reality. When the Intergovernmental Panel on Climate Change (IPCC) issued a landmark report warning of the severe consequences of climate change, prominent climate scientist Michael E. Mann tweeted, "To those who say that the #IPCC is alarmist: If anything it is the opposite. Once again, with their latest report, they have been overly conservative (i.e. erring on the side of understating/ underestimating the problem)." David Wallace-Wells, climate columnist for *New York Magazine*, summarized the report's findings, writing that "barring the arrival of dramatic new carbon-sucking technologies, which are so far from scalability at present that they are best described as fantasies of industrial absolution, it will not be possible to keep warming below two degrees Celsius—the level the new report describes as a climate catastrophe. As a planet, we are coursing along a trajectory that brings us north of four degrees by the end of the century."[3] Meteorologist Eric Holthaus tweeted with a touch of grim sarcasm, "Sorry to be harping so much on this climate change thing, but we only have 12 years to complete a total transformation of global society before we lock in irreversible planetary change for millions of years so I'm eager to get started."

Faced with this daunting reality, the majority of Republicans not only deny the problem but attack public figures who try to raise awareness about it. One of their preferred targets is former vice president Al Gore, who has spent decades on the front lines of the climate battle. Emily Atkin, staff writer at the *New Republic*, argued that the claim "Gore and his ilk are hypocrites is a classic conservative attack strategy of redirection (because it ignores the core issue of climate change) and of poisoning the well (because it attempts to discredit the message by discrediting the messenger)." Atkin wrote that "climate change advocates who don't live a carbon-neutral lifestyle aren't hypocrites because, for the most part, they're not asking you to live a carbon-neutral lifestyle. They're asking governments, utilities, energy companies, and large corporations to increase their use of renewable energy so that you can continue to live your life as you please, without contributing to global warming."[4]

Climate deniers use an array of specious arguments to defend their position, among them false equivalence—pretending that the science on climate change isn't conclusive. "I think that both sides have their own results, from their studies, and I appreciate and I respect both sides of the science," asserted Kelly Craft, U.S. Ambassador to Canada. But according to NASA, "Multiple studies published in peer-reviewed scientific journals show that 97 percent or more of actively publishing climate scientists agree: Climate-warming trends over the past century are extremely likely due to human activities."[5] The Union of Concerned Scientists (UCS) explained that signs of human impact on earth's climate "are turning up in a diverse range of records and can be seen in the ocean, in the atmosphere, and on the Earth's surface." As UCS affirmed, "Scientists agree that today's warming is primarily caused by humans putting too much carbon in the atmosphere, like when we choose to extract and burn coal, oil, and gas, or cut down and burn forests."[6]

Environmental scientist Dana Nuccitelli debunked the right-wing talking point that the tiny fraction of climate scientists who defy scientific consensus are courageous truth tellers. "Those who reject the 97% expert consensus on human-caused global warming often invoke Galileo as an example of when the scientific minority overturned the majority view. In reality, climate contrarians have almost nothing in common with Galileo, whose conclusions were based on empirical scientific evidence, supported by many scientific contemporaries, and persecuted by the religious-political establishment."[7] Stefan Rahmstorf, head of Earth system analysis at the Potsdam Institute for Climate Impact Research, tweeted that the real issue for these climate contrarians is "simple demand-supply economics. Out of the ~ 10,000 climate scientists of the world, only a handful are willing to say the kind of nonsense that fossil fuel interests like. But there is huge money behind the demand for them. -> Dream speaking fees."

Big money is behind the Republican Party's position on climate change—as it is on most issues. "The fossil fuel industry maintains its corrupt chokehold on the #Republican Party to prevent climate action," tweeted Democratic senator Sheldon Whitehouse. Twitter user Sara Dillon concurred: "It seems that the corruption of oil money is a common denominator in our main problems: corruption of our government (Trump-Putin), the rise of global oligarchs who buy control over governmental policy and the destruction of the environment." To Dillon's point, Greenpeace pointed out that the right-wing Koch brothers "have sent at least $100,343,292 directly to 84 groups denying climate change science since 1997."[8]

Indebted to the oil and gas industry, an intransigent Republican Party is preventing the majority of Americans from tackling the climate crisis. Citing a December 2018 NBC News/ *Wall Street Journal* poll, CNBC's John Harwood reported that "most Americans want action on climate change. Republicans are the exception." Harwood noted that while a large majority of Democrats and Independents believe it is time to address the crisis, "resistance comes only from the one-third of Americans who identify themselves as Republicans."[9] Pew Research Center noted that "Republicans, particularly conservatives, are highly critical of climate scientists and more likely to ascribe negative rather than positive motives to the influences shaping scientists' research."[10]

Renowned linguist Noam Chomsky blasted the Republican Party leadership, saying they are "dedicated to driving humanity off the cliff as soon as possible—in full knowledge of what they are doing." In an interview with political scientist C. J. Polychroniou, Chomsky also went after the CEOs of major banks, arguing that they "surely understand the extraordinary threat of environmental catastrophe but are increasing investment in fossil fuels because that's where the money is. Like the energy corporations, they are hardly eager to support candidates warning of the serious crimes they are committing."[11] Reddit user "And_Im_the_Devil" similarly made the case that the Republican Party "deserves to be viewed for the existential threat that it is rather than a responsible political organization. Its members deny climate change while taking money from polluters."

Among the Republican Party's most fanatical anti-environmentalists is Oklahoma senator James Inhofe, a climate denier who was described by League of Conservation

Voters president Gene Karpinski as the "original climate-denier in chief."[12] Inhofe drew widespread ridicule by throwing a snowball on the Senate floor to "prove" global warming was a hoax. Political analyst and MSNBC host Nicole Wallace called Inhofe's stunt "moronic." At the news and opinion website Mic, Tom McKay wrote that Inhofe was "a grown man who sits as the senior member of the Senate's Committee on Environment and Public Works, not a second grader turning in the worst science project ever." McKay argued that "Inhofe doesn't understand how climate works. Weather is not the same thing as climate, and the fact that it still gets cold every year does not disprove the fact that global average temperatures are increasing at an alarming pace."[13]

Conflating weather and climate isn't the worst of Inhofe's transgressions. The Republican senator has been instrumental in spreading denialist propaganda. In an interview with former Arkansas governor Mike Huckabee, Inhofe falsely claimed that "we went into a leveling-out period about eight years ago." To which Kate Sheppard, a journalist who has reported extensively on environmental issues, responded, "Nope. Sorry."[14] Speaking to right-wing radio host Eric Metaxas, Inhofe insisted that kids were being "brainwashed" in schools. In an audio excerpt published by Right Wing Watch, Inhofe said that after his granddaughter confronted him about global warming, he "did some checking" and realized that "the stuff that they teach our kids nowadays . . . you have to un-brainwash them when they get out."[15]

According to the *Washington Post*, "At least half a dozen former aides to Inhofe—and counting—have been hired into top positions at the EPA and the White House."[16] One of Inhofe's longtime friends is disgraced former Environmental Protection Agency head Scott Pruitt, the embodiment of Republican anti-environmentalism. "Pruitt is as rotten is it gets," tweeted tennis legend and political activist Martina Navratilova. Laurie David, coauthor of *The Down-to-Earth Guide to Global Warming*, said that Pruitt was "corrupt and immoral, just how trump likes them." Pruitt's history was well known before Trump tapped him as EPA administrator. "In his previous job as the attorney general of Oklahoma, he sought to use legal tools to fight environmental regulations on the oil and gas companies that are a major part of the state's economy," the *New York Times* reported.[17]

Once in place as head of the EPA, Pruitt turned the agency over to big polluters. "We no longer have an Environmental Protection Agency. It's now the Environmental Destruction Agency," writer Kath Barnes tweeted. A full inventory of Pruitt's malfeasance would consume an entire book, but PBS provided a handy summary of his destructive acts: He "played a key role in Trump's decision to withdraw from the Paris Climate Agreement . . . signed a formal proposal to repeal the Clean Power Plan . . . announced that the EPA would review fuel emissions standards . . . ordered a delay of a new regulation on methane leaks for two years . . . denied a petition from the Natural Resources Defense Council and the Pesticide

Action Network North America calling for a ban of the pesticide chlorpyrifos . . . suspended the Clean Water Rule for two years . . . tried delaying the designation of areas that met the National Ambient Air Quality Standards for ozone."[18]

Pruitt's corruption shocked even veteran political observers. *Slate*'s chief political correspondent Jamelle Bouie wrote that Pruitt "was allowed to perpetrate a staggering level of self-dealing," adding that his "list of scandals is extensive and almost unbelievable."[19] Author and investigative reporter David Cay Johnston tweeted, "Scott Pruitt clearly thinks he is beyond accountability." When Pruitt finally resigned, Rep. Pramila Jayapal tweeted, "I began demanding Scott Pruitt's firing months ago. Today, the #BootPruitt campaign got RESULTS. That it took so long—scandal after scandal after scandal—speaks volumes about the tolerance for corruption and misconduct in the Trump administration." But Pruitt's replacement, former coal-industry lobbyist Andrew R. Wheeler, wasn't much of an improvement. "Scott Pruitt's replacement has been in the job for less than a month. He's already facing ethics scrutiny. Corruption, right from the beginning," tweeted "The Hummingbird," a popular resistance account. Former Democratic congressional candidate Omar Vaid called the transition from Pruitt to Wheeler "EPA Whac-a-mole," writing that Wheeler is "an Oklahoma coal lobbyist who spent his life opposing environmental protection." MSNBC host Chris Hayes tweeted, "Andrew Wheeler as the head of EPA is the equivalent of a tobacco lobbyist heading up HHS."

In September 2018, ThinkProgress reported that 1,600 EPA employees quit the agency after Trump took office, citing "frustration with Trump's radically anti-environment agenda."[20] On the right, the exodus was cheered. When the right-wing media outlet *Human Events* posted on Facebook about EPA staff departures under Pruitt, commenters were elated:

> When the heat is turned up, the cockroaches run. —Linda Greene

> Awesome, keep up the good work Mr. Pruitt! EPA jobs, as with most government jobs, are nothing more than welfare with a title. —Dan Bissonnette

> Great news! Time to end the EPA environazi's power! —Joe Elms

> God bless us everyone! Over 14,000 EPA employees still remain, which about 13,826 too many, but hey, hope & change, baby! Hope & change. —David Kaiser

> Thank you lord. This is one overreacting and over reaching Government agency that needs to be Gone. Along with the IRS, the BLM, The Dept. of Education, think we can pay off our national debt. In a heartbeat. —Nelson James

The Republican Party's aggressive anti-environmentalism highlights the nexus between climate denial and right-wing extremism. Michael Barnard, who writes and consults about climate disruption, argued that "strong evidence has emerged from multiple peer-reviewed and published studies that if you scratch a white, male, far-right nationalist, you'll find a denier of climate science as well."[21] A Redditor named "Leocto" wrote that climate change "is an *international* problem that needs *international* solutions and *international* cooperation, which is exactly the reason why *nationalist* parties and groups hate it so much and will forever deny it even if it hits them in the face. Both 'international' and 'cooperation' are words (ultra-)nationalists are allergic to. Combine them, and they go apeshit."

Climate denial is part of a wider pattern of right-wing conspiracy-mongering. Surgical oncologist David Gorski tweeted that denialists "share similarities, be they antivaxers, creationists, climate science deniers, Holocaust deniers, HIV/AIDS denialists, etc. They use the same techniques to deny, downplay, and obfuscate conclusions they don't like." Australian cognitive scientist Stephan Lewandowsky—who studies how myths and misinformation spread—told reporter Alex Seitz-Wald, "A conspiracy theory is immune to evidence, and that can pretty well serve as the definition of one. If you reject evidence, or reinterpret the evidence to be confirmation of your theory, or you ignore mountains of evidence to focus on just one thing, you're probably a conspiracy theorist. We call that a self-sealing nature of reasoning."[22]

Drawing on Lewandowsky's research, Vox's Jane Coaston explained, "Trying to disprove a conspiracy theory thus usually only serves to reinforce it."[23] Coaston placed climate denial in the wider context of conspiracies like QAnon (an outlandish belief which took root on 4chan and caught fire on social media). The *Washington Post*'s Molly Roberts summarized the QAnon plot:

> President Trump isn't under investigation; he is only pretending to be, as part of a countercoup to restore power to the people after more than a century of governmental control by a globalist cabal. Also, there are pedophiles. A figure named 'Q,' who supposedly possesses Q-level security clearance, disperses 'crumbs' that 'bakers' bring together to create a 'dough' of synthesized information. (This is not how baking works, but that seems the least of our worries.) Because Q is the 17th letter in the alphabet and 17 is also a number Trump has said a few times, among other clearly-not-coincidences, he is the real deal, not an Internet troll engaged in an elaborate example of live-action role-play.[24]

While it may be tempting to dismiss these wild conspiracies as fringe ideas, conspiracy-mongering *costs lives*. Violent attacks have been carried out by white males radicalized in far-right forums that traffic in conspiracy theories. And conspiracies like QAnon have gained credence among MAGA voters, who have shown up at Trump rallies wearing "Q" T-shirts. Professors Leah Payne and Brian Doak, hosts of the *Weird Religion* podcast, explained that "Trump-based conspiracies floating around on the right" have "a deep religious impulse" at their core. Payne and Doak wrote that "conspiracists exude confidence that Trump is fulfilling his campaign promises and God's plan for the world, which many Trump supporters see as one and the same."[25] "QAnon + Scripture = Evangelical Christianity," tweeted entrepreneur Lauren Santo Domingo.

Climate denial may end up being the deadliest of right-wing conspiracies, hindering our ability to act on what amounts to a global emergency. Bob Ward, policy and communications director at the Grantham Research Institute on Climate Change and the Environment, tweeted that "history will judge harshly the politicians, particularly in right-wing Parties, in the US, Canada, UK and Australia who still promoted climate change denial in 2018, in spite of overwhelming scientific evidence, because of ideology and vested interests."

In 1965, American Petroleum Institute head Frank N. Ikard issued a prescient warning that went largely unheeded: "There is still time to save the world's peoples from the catastrophic consequence of pollution, but time is running out." When Ikard raised the alarm, it would be "another decade before the phrase 'global warming' would appear for the first time in a peer-reviewed study," wrote Sharon Kelly at *DeSmogBlog*.[26] More than a half century later, most Americans know that time is running out to mitigate the worst effects of climate change.

That much is no longer in doubt. What *is* in doubt is whether the GOP and its right-wing media allies will ever take their heads out of the sand. And their hands out of big oil's pockets.

There is a popular adage among environmentalists that "we do not inherit the earth from our ancestors, we borrow it from our children." The Republican Party is sinking us deep into debt, a debt to the future we may not be able to repay. If there is a ray of hope, it is that a new generation of activists is taking on the climate fight. As Aaron Huertas, strategic communications director for Swing Left, tweeted, "A whole generation coming up behind us is ready to lead the way on climate. Let them lead us."

One of those new leaders is fifteen-year-old Swedish climate activist Greta Thunberg, whose widely praised speech at the COP24 climate summit included a pointed warning: "Our civilization is being sacrificed for the opportunity of a very small number of people to continue making enormous amounts of money . . . We have run out of excuses and we are running out of time. We have come here to let you know that change is coming, whether you like it or not. The real power belongs to the people."[27] In the U.S., Alexandria Ocasio-Cortez, a rising political star and the youngest woman ever elected to Congress, has worked with a new generation of protestors demanding a Green New Deal, a transformative proposal to simultaneously address climate change and income inequality. "Fight for the planet, fight for our lives," Ocasio-Cortez tweeted.

FINDING OUR MORAL COMPASS

*It is easy for us to lose ourselves in details in
endeavoring to grasp and comprehend the real condition
of a mass of human beings. We often forget that each
unit in the mass is a throbbing human soul.*
—W.E.B. DuBois, *The Souls of Black Folk*

When blue Americans step onto the digital battlefield, they face
a formidable foe: a dedicated and motivated Republican base,
called to arms by an extremist Republican Party and amplified by a powerful right-wing media machine. These digital
combatants will have to fight the Republicans on multiple
fronts, opposing their xenophobic immigration policies and
abuse of migrant families; their ruthless efforts to sabotage the
Affordable Care Act with no plan to replace it; their protection
racket for oligarchs, stealing from the poor to give to the rich;
their death pact with the NRA, where American schoolchildren
are treated as little more than collateral damage; their coziness
with big polluters, poisoning our planet to line their pockets

with oil money; their dime-store patriotism, attacking the FBI and intelligence community to cover for Russia's assault on our democracy; their constant crowing about "respecting the flag" while veterans go homeless; their lack of honor, cheating to win campaigns by suppressing the vote; their theft of a Supreme Court seat and confirmation of an accused sexual assaulter (and serial perjurer) to the highest court, denigrating the #MeToo movement and sending a chilling message to survivors; their cynical attempts to manipulate voters with focus-grouped narratives cooked up in billionaire-funded think tanks; their faux populism and rampant hypocrisy; and their smug moralizing as they equivocate on Nazis and embolden white supremacists.

And in turn, red Americans will accuse Democrats of wanting to open our borders to dangerous "illegals"; of supporting big government and "socialized medicine"; of trying to repeal the Second Amendment and scheming to confiscate their guns; of disrespecting the flag and looking down on them as "deplorables." They'll diagnose Democrats with Trump Derangement Syndrome and ridicule them for believing the "liberal media." And they'll "whatabout" them on abortion, saying Democrats have no moral standing because they support "murdering babies."

These bitter social media clashes are now a full-blown Digital Civil War, a relentless barrage of personal attacks, threats, harassment, and hate, where rational discourse and reasoned debate are the first casualties. The seemingly unbridgeable divide between the warring parties has led some political observers to suggest that it's time to abandon our failing political union, to split America in two. Kevin Baker, contributing editor at the *New Republic*, proposed a "bluexit," telling red Americans, "Go ahead, keep on voting against your own economic interests to satisfy your need to control other people's bodies, sex lives, and recreational habits. We'll be creating cities and states that will defend gay marriage, a woman's right to choose, and sensible gun control against your intrusive federal judiciary."[1] MSNBC host Joy Reid convened a panel to discuss Baker's idea, asking why blue states should keep subsidizing "a part of the country that is red seemingly permanently."[2]

But breaking up is not what most Americans want. They want to defend their values *without* ripping the nation apart. That won't be easy, not if we can't agree to some basic standards of decency. Take immigration. It's hard to imagine a more barbaric policy than forcibly snatching terrified children from their parents and locking them in frigid holding cells, where they are getting sick and dying. If we can't agree that this practice is morally abhorrent, how can we come together as a nation? Yet right-wing Republicans, including some in the GOP leadership, callously claim that we have to do these terrible things to deter "illegals." They'll say Obama caged children too and liberals didn't complain then. And yes, unaccompanied migrant children were placed in cages under Obama— and it was a travesty that warranted wider condemnation. But what Trump and the GOP have done is exponentially worse, separating asylum-seeking families by force for the "crime" of wanting a safer life in America.

Republicans argue that we have to enforce our laws. Of *course* we do. We need a comprehensive and fair immigration policy. But solving the problem requires cooperation and compassion, not brutality and inhumanity. It requires empathy for women and children escaping gang violence and domestic abuse, who see America as a beacon of hope. Some Democratic activists scoff that we can't expect empathy from MAGA voters because they don't see migrants as fully human. And Republicans argue that if parents don't want their kids taken from them, they shouldn't show up at our border. To which I respond that showing up at our border is *exactly* how you seek asylum. And so the fight goes.

The deep animosity among activists on both sides of the divide has made us caricatures to each other. And digital media exacerbates that sense of dislocation and disconnection. Van Jones, the CNN commentator, complained that many liberals "look at the red states the same way that colonizers once viewed developing countries. All they see is a bunch of backward, unwashed, uneducated heathens who need to be converted to the NPR religion and force-fed kale until they see the light."[3] I disagree. In my experience, it's not so much that liberals want to "convert" Republicans, it's that blue Americans are tired of being subjected to regressive GOP policies foisted on them by a loud and radicalized right-wing minority.

America may not yet be broken, but it is most certainly breaking. The gulf between increasingly extremist Republicans and increasingly frustrated Democrats impedes meaningful progress on a range of critical issues—leading to a perpetual deadlock that costs lives. Consider gun violence, the scourge that took nearly forty thousand precious American souls in 2017. I grew up a hunter and gun owner. I lived in a war zone and received military training during my teens. (No, I don't think the "AR" in AR-15 stands for "assault rifle.") I survived years of urban warfare and I witnessed every manner of savagery. But I *never* imagined, not in my worst nightmare, that I'd come back home to see American schoolchildren being massacred in classrooms, to see innocent civilians being slaughtered in churches, synagogues, clubs, and theaters.

How can anyone's first reaction to mass murder be "protect the Second Amendment" instead of "protect the innocent?" How can people vote for politicians who shrug off the atrocity of school massacres? Mitch McConnell said it was a "darn shame" that there isn't much the Senate can do to prevent the scourge of gun violence. That callousness is typical of GOP officials. If Republicans aren't willing to let go of NRA talking points to protect American kids from being shot to death in their classrooms, what *is* their moral code?

Journalism professor Christian Christensen tweeted that the "moral perversity that allows one to think that universal healthcare is tyranny but dead school children are the price of freedom is what is corroding the soul of the United States."

He's absolutely right. Our values are our priorities. What we stand for, and what we stand against, makes us who we are as a people. We *can* fix the gun violence problem. Other nations protect their children. It's outrageous and unpatriotic to claim that we can't. David Frum, the political commentator, argued that "the first step toward correcting a social wrong is opening people's eyes to see that wrong." Frum said we're facing "a moral reckoning and awakening," and "that while the awakening may often come tragically slow, it does come in time, with all the power of justice delayed but not denied."[4] The reckoning doesn't mean we should be confiscating guns and repealing the Second Amendment. What it means is that we have no choice but to tackle this unmitigated tragedy together. Not by arming teachers, not by throwing more guns at the problem, but by finding common-sense solutions. And thankfully, we're starting to see signs of progress.

The massacre at Marjory Stoneman Douglas High School in Parkland, Florida, is seen as a turning point in the gun-reform fight. Parkland survivors have used social media to mobilize, organize, and inspire people across the country. (Notably, one of those survivors, Emma González, has amassed more than twice as many Twitter followers as the NRA.) The Giffords Law Center called the events of 2018 a "tectonic shift" on gun safety.[5] Good people are making a difference at the state and local levels. But Republican leaders and their NRA handlers are still stonewalling. What will it take for the GOP and the gun lobby to let go of the idea that it's about *them*, and not the victims?

The fight over abortion is another raging political and social conflict that requires common sense and compassion, not absolutism. So many anti-choicers use the issue as a moral cudgel against those of us who support a woman's right to decide what happens inside her body. But questions of life, personhood, and conception are impossibly difficult. Bioethicists, medical professionals, and legal experts have spent lifetimes debating them. Anyone who says abortion is a clear-cut ethical issue is deluding themselves. When my wife and I learned that our first pregnancy together was ectopic, it was absolutely crushing. And when we were told by her obstetrician that she needed emergency surgery to save her life—and that the faint heartbeat we heard inside her would be silenced—the tears streamed down, and years later, they still do. That is precisely why I believe the morally correct thing to do is to respect a woman's freedom of choice. The fact that the issue is so intractable, that the ethical questions are so profound, is one of the strongest arguments in favor of choice. When so much is at stake and so many sincere, decent people have diametrically opposed views, it is not the government's place to impose its will on a woman. It never is. Christians may claim abortion violates their religious code, but there's no valid scriptural basis for that belief. *Nowhere* in the Bible is abortion explicitly prohibited.

Another issue that demands moral clarity is the Republican Party's brazen attempts to steal elections through gerrymandering and voter suppression. Sherrilyn Ifill, president and director-counsel of the NAACP Legal Defense Fund, wrote that there is "an effort to rig the game to ensure that one side never loses. The permanent gerrymander is a key feature."[6] These attacks on the pillars of our democracy should alarm *every* citizen—free and fair elections are our bulwark against despotism. As Christina Reynolds, vice president of communications at EMILY's List, tweeted, "If your way of winning elected office is to ensure certain people don't vote, you don't deserve the office. Period." When Democrats took control of the House in 2019, their first bill was the anti-corruption For the People Act (H.R. 1). Ari Berman, author of *Give Us the Ballot: The Modern Struggle for Voting Rights in America*, reported that the bill would "expand voting rights and curb the influence of money in politics."[7] Former White House ethics czar Norman L. Eisen tweeted, "Before we can retake the mantle of defending democracy around the world, we have to begin by restoring the promise of American democracy at home. #HR1 is a powerful signal to our citizens and to the world that our constitutional democracy WILL recover." H.R. 1 is a promising start, but we have a long way to go before we can fix our broken election system.

On issue after contentious issue, we have to use our own judgment, conscience, and common sense to figure out—and to do—the right thing. We don't have to be scientists to know that spewing pollution into the atmosphere is harmful. We don't have to be mathematicians or policy experts to understand that millions of people without health insurance is bad.

We don't have to be economists to see that the rich are getting richer and that giving tax breaks to billionaires is repugnant. We don't have to rely on others for our basic moral code—not our political leaders, not our religious leaders, and certainly not the media.

When we clash over our ideals and principles, it shouldn't be a contest of who can be the meanest or snarkiest, who can humiliate and "dunk on" the other, who can join the biggest and angriest mob. It should be about upholding our values and protecting the most vulnerable among us. The digital battlefield is brutal. Women, and particularly women of color, are subjected to a torrent of verbal abuse. But they fight because they care, and because their lives depend on it. Author and educator Dr. Eve L. Ewing tweeted, "Do you know how tiring it is to have to tell your loved ones that random people you've never met hate you and threaten you on the internet for literally no reason and that it should indeed be taken seriously, without feeling like a primadonna or like you're acting paranoid . . . Sick of the wasted time. Sick of the fear." She's not alone. People are stressed and scared. They're worried that some of our fellow citizens have become unreachable. As author Roxane Gay put it, "You cannot reason with people who don't recognize the humanity in all of us."[8]

Good people want to make things better for those around them. It's part of life's purpose. And as Americans, we have a special responsibility to uphold our nation's highest aspirations, to make our republic a model of justice, fairness, and equality. *That's* what being a patriot is, not putting a flag decal on your bumper or berating athletes for kneeling.

Most Americans think Washington is out of touch with their concerns: a 2018 Pew Research survey found that only a third of the public had a favorable view of the federal government.[9] And having worked on political campaigns in D.C., I know that Beltway culture is often the equivalent of a schoolyard, with its petty rivalries, insiderism, clans and cliques—except the fate of the country is at stake. But even if the Washington establishment deserves the criticism it gets, the right's hostility is misdirected. The problem isn't EPA staffers who want to protect our air and water, it's a Republican-run White House that hands the EPA to big polluters. It isn't Democratic lawmakers MAGA voters should be wary of, it's GOP leaders like Mitch McConnell, Lindsey Graham, Mike Pence, Ted Cruz, and Donald Trump, who pretend to care about working people while serving the whims of their ultrawealthy patrons.

And yes, there are corrupt Democrats and unprincipled liberals—no party or politician is perfect—but we shouldn't be lulled by false equivalence. Nothing in American life is more of a threat to our democracy than the Republican Party's lurch to the far right. Jesse Lee, former special assistant to President Obama, tweeted that the GOP "has largely detached itself from the American democratic value system." It is a party without moral bearings, lacking integrity and honor, doing the bidding of oligarchs while coddling white supremacists. Former

U.S. Navy JAG Pam Keith tweeted that today's GOP "is truly cruel. There is not an ounce of human empathy or compassion between them. They get off on terrorizing, demeaning, destabilizing, marginalizing, rejecting & actually harming the most vulnerable people in the world."

The triumvirate of right-wing media, right-wing megadonors, and a right-wing Republican Party is an existential threat to the United States of America, undermining the norms, values, and principles that define the nation. Even before the rise of Trump, Thomas E. Mann, a senior fellow at the Brookings Institution, wrote that Republicans "have become a radical insurgency—ideologically extreme, contemptuous of the inherited policy regime, scornful of compromise, unpersuaded by conventional understanding of facts, evidence, and science; and dismissive of the legitimacy of their political opposition."[10] As journalism professor Jeff Jarvis put it, "The GOP is moving over the crackpot cliff."

In the eighteenth century, the Enlightenment philosopher Voltaire warned: "those who can make you believe absurdities, can make you commit atrocities." For blue Americans in the twenty-first century—and for principled patriots across the ideological spectrum—the Digital Civil War is about preventing that descent into tyranny by confronting the far-right menace before it's too late.

NOTES

PROLOGUE

1   Frank Bruni, "Donald Trump's Radical Honesty," *New York Times*, January 18, 2018, https://www.nytimes.com/2018/01/19/opinion/sunday/donald-trump-lies-honesty.html.

2   *Anderson Cooper 360°*, CNN, August 23, 2018.

3   Thomas L. Friedman, "The American Civil War, Part II," *New York Times*, October 2, 2018, https://www.nytimes.com/2018/10/02/opinion/the-american-civil-war-part-ii.html.

4   Colin Moynihan and Ali Winston, "Far-Right Proud Boys Reeling After Arrests and Scrutiny," *New York Times*, December 23, 2018, https://www.nytimes.com/2018/12/23/nyregion/gavin-mcinnes-proud-boys-nypd.html.

5   "Michael Savage: 'It's a High Probability' That Serial Bombings Are 'a False Flag to Gain Sympathy,'" Media Matters for America, October 24, 2018, https://www.mediamatters.org/video/2018/10/24/michael-savage-its-high-probability-serial-bombings-are-false-flag-gain-sympathy/221832.

6   Rush Limbaugh, "There Are No Coincidences with the Clintons," iHeart Radio, October 24, 2018, https://news.iheart.com/featured/rush-limbaugh/content/2018-10-24-rush-limbaugh-blog-there-are-no-coincidences-with-the-clintons/.

7   Jim Hoft, "LIBERAL MEDIA OUTRAGED That Bouncer-'Bomber' Story Won't Sway Trump Voters . . . and That CNN Still Sucks," Gateway Pundit, October 27, 2018, https://www.the gatewaypundit.com/2018/10/liberal-media-outraged-that -bouncer-bomber-story-wont-sway-trump-voters-and-that-cnn -still-sucks/.

8   Anti-Defamation League, *Murder and Extremism in the United States in 2016*, 2017, https://www.adl.org/resources/reports /murder-and-extremism-in-the-united-states-in-2016.

9   United States Government Accountability Office, *Countering Violent Extremism*, April 2017, www.gao.gov/assets/690 /683984.pdf.

10 Wesley Lowery, Kimberly Kindy, and Andrew Ba Tran, "In the United States, Right-Wing Violence is on the Rise," *Washington Post*, November 25, 2018, https://www.washingtonpost.com /national/in-the-united-states-right-wing-violence-is-on-the -rise/2018/11/25/61f7f24a-deb4-11e8-85df-7a6b4d25cfbb_story .html?noredirect=on&utm_term=.a999d0aded97.

11 Sarah Kendzior, "Kavanaugh's Appointment Isn't a Step Backward. It's a Head-First Plunge into an Ugly Past," *Globe and Mail*, October 6, 2018, https://www.theglobeandmail.com/amp /opinion/article-kavanaughs-appointment-isnt-a-step-backward -its-a-head-first/.

12 Public Citizen (@Public_Citizen), "While everyone's been focused on Trump's antics, nine states with a history of racial discrimination have been quietly but aggressively removing voters from the," Twitter, October 6, 2018, https://twitter.com /Public_Citizen/status/1048703951959408641.

13 Michiko Kakutani, introduction to *The Death of Truth: Notes on Falsehood in the Age of Trump* (New York: Tim Duggan Books, 2018), introduction.

14   Roger J. Katz and Stephen L. D'Andrilli, "Political Left &
      Political Right Wage a Modern-Day Civil War For America's
      Soul," *AmmoLand*, May 17, 2018, https://www.ammoland.com
      /2018/05/political-left-political-right-wage-a-modern-day-civil
      -war-for-americas-soul/#axzz5apFKvFa6.

15   Elie Wiesel, preface to *Night* (New York: Hill and Wang, 2006),
      preface.

16   P. W. Singer and Emerson T. Brooking, *LikeWar: The
      Weaponization of Social Media* (New York: Houghton Mifflin
      Harcourt, 2018), 19.

17   Thomas E. Ricks, "What a New U.S. Civil War Might Look Like,"
      Foreign Policy, October 10, 2017, https://foreignpolicy.com
      /2017/10/10/what-a-new-u-s-civil-war-might-look-like/.

18   R. J. Reinhart, "Record U.S. Partisan Divide on Views of the
      NRA," Gallup, June 28, 2018, https://news.gallup.com/poll
      /236315/record-partisan-divide-views-nra.aspx.

19   "Ipsos Poll Conducted for Reuters: Russia Poll 7.18.2018," Ipsos
      Public Affairs, https://www.ipsos.com/sites/default/files
      /ct/news/documents/2018-07/2018_reuters_tracking_-_russia
      _7_18_2018.pdf.

20   "Public Opinion on Abortion," Pew Research Center, October 15,
      2018, http://www.pewforum.org/fact-sheet/public-opinion-on
      -abortion/.

21   "Little Partisan Agreement on the Pressing Problems Facing the
      U.S.," Pew Research Center, October 15, 2018, http://www
      .people-press.org/wp-content/uploads/sites/4/2018/10/Mid
      term-Report-for-release.pdf.

22   Martin Baron, "Remarks by Washington Post Executive Editor
      Martin Baron at the 2018 Fourth Estate Awards," *Washington
      Post*, November 30, 2018, https://www.washingtonpost.com/pr
      /2018/11/30/remarks-by-washington-post-executive-editor

-martin-baron-fourth-estate-awards/?noredirect=on&utm
_term=.071d54e306f4.

23   Norman Ornstein, "Yes, Polarization Is Asymmetric—and
      Conservatives Are Worse," *Atlantic*, June 19, 2014, https://www
      .theatlantic.com/politics/archive/2014/06/yes-polarization-is
      -asymmetric-and-conservatives-are-worse/373044/.

24   Julian E. Zelizer, "How Conservatives Won the Battle over the
      Courts," *Atlantic*, July 7, 2018, https://www.theatlantic.com
      /ideas/archive/2018/07/how-conservatives-won-the-battle-over
      -the-courts/564533/.

25   Tayari Jones, "There's Nothing Virtuous About Finding
      Common Ground," *Time*, October 25, 2018, http://time.com
      /5434381/tayari-jones-moral-middle-myth/.

26   Yochai Benkler, Robert Faris, Hal Roberts, and Ethan
      Zuckerman, "Study: Breitbart-Led Right-Wing Media Ecosystem
      Altered Broader Media Agenda," *Columbia Journalism Review*,
      March 3, 2017, https://www.cjr.org/analysis/breitbart-media
      -trump-harvard-study.php.

27   Nolan McCarty, "What We Know and Don't Know About Our
      Polarized Politics," *Washington Post*, January 8, 2014, https://
      www.washingtonpost.com/news/monkey-cage/wp
      /2014/01/08/what-we-know-and-dont-know-about-our
      -polarized-politics/?noredirect=on&utm_term=.f7a541a551b9.

28   James Baldwin, "AS MUCH TRUTH AS ONE CAN BEAR; To Speak
      Out About the World as It Is, Says James Baldwin, Is the Writer's
      Job as Much of the Truth as One Can Bear," *New York Times*,
      January 14, 1962, https://www.nytimes.com/1962/01/14
      /archives/as-much-truth-as-one-can-bear-to-speak-out-about
      -the-world-as-it-is.html.

29 John Stuart Mill, "The Contest in America," *Fraser's Magazine,* February 1862.

CHAPTER 1

1 Toni Morrison, "Making America White Again," *New Yorker,* November 21, 2016, https://www.newyorker.com/magazine /2016/11/21/making-america-white-again.

2 Elizabeth Cady Stanton, *The Selected Papers of Elizabeth Cady Stanton and Susan B. Anthony: In the School of Anti-Slavery, 1840 to 1866* (New Jersey: Rutgers University Press, 1997), 132.

3 Eugene Robinson, "'Real' Americans Are a Myth. Don't You Dare Buy It," *Washington Post,* May 14, 2018, https://www .washingtonpost.com/opinions/real-americans-are-a-myth -dont-you-dare-buy-it/2018/05/14/b4c3099e-57a3-11e8-8836- a4a123c359ab_story.html?noredirect=on&utm_term= .814847698738.

4 Jennifer Rubin, "The Real 'Real America,'" *Washington Post,* November 9, 2018, https://www.washingtonpost.com /news/opinions/wp/2018/11/09/the-real-real-america /?noredirect=on&utm_term=.a398bd08cd45.

5 Frank Miniter, "The Myth of Flyover Country's 'Real America,'" *National Review,* December 20, 2016, https://www .nationalreview.com/2016/12/real-america-myth-republicans -need-drop-damaging-label/.

6 Nell Irvin Painter, *The History of White People* (New York: W. W. Norton, 2010), 363.

7 Kathy Frankovic, "Republicans See Little Need for the Russia Investigation," YouGov, December 8, 2017, https://today.yougov

.com/topics/politics/articles-reports/2017/12/08/republicans-see
-little-need-russia-investigation.

8   Ian Reifowitz, "Wanna Know Why Republicans Can't Give Up
     Calling Obama 'Not American'? They've Got Nothing Else,"
     HuffPost, July 28, 2014, https://www.huffingtonpost.com/ian
     -reifowitz/wanna-know-why-republican_b_5627073.html.

9   Greg Sargent, "Trump's Hate and Lies Are Inciting Extremists.
     Just Ask the Analyst Who Warned Us," *Washington Post*, October
     29, 2018, https://www.washingtonpost.com/blogs
     /plum-line/wp/2018/10/29/trumps-hate-and-lies-are
     -emboldening-extremists-just-ask-the-analyst-who-warned-us
     /?noredirect=on&utm_term=.88db3e5b91de.

10   Jason Stanley, "The Mythic Past," chap. 1 in *How Fascism Works:
     The Politics of Us and Them* (New York: Random House, 2018), 3.

11   Louis Hyman, "The Myth of Main Street," *New York Times*, April
     8, 2017, https://www.nytimes.com/2017/04/08/opinion/sunday
     /the-myth-of-main-street.html.

12   Robert Wuthnow, *The Left Behind: Decline and Rage in Rural
     America* (Princeton, NJ: Princeton University Press, 2018), 3.

13   Jed Kolko, "'Normal America' Is Not a Small Town of White
     People," FiveThirtyEight, April 28, 2016, https://fivethirtyeight
     .com/features/normal-america-is-not-a-small-town-of-white
     -people/.

14   Alec MacGillis and ProPublica, "The Original Underclass,"
     Atlantic, September 2016, https://www.theatlantic.com
     /magazine/archive/2016/09/the-original-underclass/492731/.

15   Tamara Draut, "Understanding the Working Class" (New York:
     Demos, April 16, 2018), https://www.demos.org/publication
     /understanding-working-class.

16   Victoria A. Brownworth, "Women Are the Working Class," DAME, April 12, 2018, https://www.damemagazine.com /2018/04/12/women-are-the-working-class/.

17   Susan B. Glasser and Glenn Thrush, "What's Going On with America's White People?" *Politico,* September/October 2016, https://www.politico.com/magazine/story/2016/09/problems -white-people-america-society-class-race-214227.

18   Nancy Isenberg, *White Trash: The 400-Year Untold History of Class in America* (New York: Viking, 2016), 275.

19   Callum Borchers, "Joe Biden Says Democrats Have Stopped Talking to White, Working-Class Voters," *Washington Post,* July 27, 2016, https://www.washingtonpost.com/news/the-fix/wp/2016 /07/27/joe-biden-says-democrats-have-stopped-talking-to-white -working-class-voters/?noredirect=on&utm_term=.cb507a119f0a.

20   Nicholas Carnes and Noam Lupu, "It's Time to Bust the Myth: Most Trump Voters Were Not Working Class," *Washington Post,* June 5, 2017, https://www.washingtonpost.com/news/monkey -cage/wp/2017/06/05/its-time-to-bust-the-myth-most-trump -voters-were-not-working-class/?noredirect=on&utm_term= .b61a2ba9a47e.

21   Derek Thompson, "The Dangerous Myth That Hillary Clinton Ignored the Working Class," *Atlantic,* December 5, 2016, https: //www.theatlantic.com/business/archive/2016/12/hillary -clinton-working-class/509477/.

22   Jeremy W. Peters, "As Critics Assail Trump, His Supporters Dig In Deeper," *New York Times,* June 23, 2018, https://www.nytimes .com/2018/06/23/us/politics/republican-voters-trump.html.

23   Martin Savidge, Tristan Smith, and Emanuella Grinberg, "What Trump Supporters Think of Family Separations at the Border,"

CNN, June 19, 2018, https://www.cnn.com/2018/06/19/us /trump-voters-family-separation/index.html.

24 Matt Flegenheimer, "After Putin Meeting, Trump Voters Mostly Dig In. But Cracks Are Showing," *New York Times,* July 17, 2018, https://www.nytimes.com/2018/07/17/us/politics/republican -voters-trump-putin.html.

25 Josh Hafner and Susan Page, "President Trump's Voters Remain Loyal, Even as Mueller's Russia Investigation Intensifies," *USA Today,* August 7, 2018, https://www.usatoday.com/story /news/2018/08/07/trump-voters-reject-reports-russia-inter ference-mueller-investigation/887478002/.

26 Heather Long and Scott Clement, "Trump Voters Hit Hard by Tariffs Are Standing by Him—for Now," *Washington Post,* July 12, 2018, https://www.washingtonpost.com/business/2018/07/12 /trump-voters-hit-hard-by-tariffs-are-standing-by-him-now /?noredirect=on&utm_term=.027f4c4cd816.

27 Tom Polansek, "Iowa Farmers Wary of Aid, Trade Wars but Still Turn Out for Trump," Reuters, July 26, 2018, https://www.reuters .com/article/us-usa-trade-farmers-iowa/iowa-farmers-wary-of -aid-trade-wars-but-still-turn-out-for-trump-idUSKBN1KG36Z.

28 "Their Industries Are Hurting, but Voters Still Back Trump's Trade Policy," NBC, July 1, 2018, https://www.msnbc.com/kasie -dc/watch/their-industries-are-hurting-but-voters-still-back -trump-s-trade-policy-1268162627784.

29 Debbie Elliott, "Voters in Florida's Panhandle Still Have Faith in Trump's Foreign Policy," NPR, July 20, 2018, https://www.npr .org/2018/07/20/630921351/voters-in-floridas-panhandle-still -have-faith-in-trumps-foreign-policy.

30 Noah Berlatsky, "Enough Already with the 'Trump Voters Still Like Trump' Stories," HuffPost, July 20, 2018, https://www

.huffingtonpost.com/entry/opinion-berlatsky-trump-coverage
_us_5b50ee0ae4b0b15aba8cea6b.

31   Oliver Willis (@owillis), "Where are our heartland diner stories?
Our profiles of surging voters who "upset the status quo" with
"maverick politicians"? How come voters in blue states . . . ,"
Twitter, November 17, 2018, https://twitter.com/owillis/status
/1063789733757820928.

32   Trip Gabriel, "As Suburban Women Turn to Democrats, Many
Suburban Men Stand with Trump," *New York Times*, October 13,
2018, https://www.nytimes.com/2018/10/13/us/politics/trump
-suburban-men-ohio.html.

33   German Lopez, "The Past Year of Research Has Made It
Very Clear: Trump Won Because of Racial Resentment," Vox,
December 15, 2017, https://www.vox.com/identities
/2017/12/15/16781222/trump-racism-economic-anxiety-study.

34   Niraj Chokshi, "Trump Voters Driven by Fear of Losing Status,
Not Economic Anxiety, Study Finds," *New York Times*, April 24,
2018, https://www.nytimes.com/2018/04/24/us/politics/trump
-economic-anxiety.html.

35   *Morning Joe*, MSNBC, October 31, 2018.

36   Sabrina Tavernise, "Why the Announcement of a Looming
White Minority Makes Demographers Nervous," *New York
Times*, November 22, 2018, https://www.nytimes.com
/2018/11/22/us/white-americans-minority-population.html.

37   Michael Harriot, "How the Republican Party Became the Party
of Racism," The Root, July 23, 2018, https://www.theroot
.com/how-the-republican-party-became-the-party-of-racism
-1827779221.

38   Dahleen Glanton, "Why Trump Supporters Feel So
Misunderstood," *Chicago Tribune*, August 2, 2018, https://www

.chicagotribune.com/news/columnists/glanton/ct-met-dahleen
-glanton-trump-voters-misunderstood-20180801-story.html.

39   Joshua Zeitz, "Does the White Working Class Really Vote
Against Its Own Interests?" *Politico,* December 31, 2017, https:
//www.politico.com/magazine/story/2017/12/31/trump-white
-working-class-history-216200.

40   Jordan B Peterson, "Stregthen the Individual." Filmed March 11,
2017 in Ottawa. YouTube video, https://www.youtube.com
/watch?time_continue=3136&v=_UL-SdOhwek

41   Carol Anderson, prologue to *White Rage: The Unspoken Truth of
Our Racial Divide* (New York: Bloomsbury, 2018), prologue.

42   Don Gonyea, "Majority of White Americans Say They Believe
Whites Face Discrimination," NPR, October 24, 2017, https:
//www.npr.org/2017/10/24/559604836/majority-of-white
-americans-think-theyre-discriminated-against.

43   Juliet Hooker, *Race and the Politics of Solidarity* (New York: Oxford
University Press, 2009), 51.

44   Michele Norris, "As America Changes, Some Anxious Whites
Feel Left Behind," *National Geographic,* April 2018, https://www
.nationalgeographic.com/magazine/2018/04/race-rising-anxiety
-white-america/.

CHAPTER 2

1   Samuel Taylor Coleridge, *Biographia Literaria* (New York: Leavitt
Lord, 1834), 174.

2   Henry Farrell, "Blame Fox, Not Facebook, for Fake News,"
Washington Post, November 6, 2018, https://www.washingtonpost
.com/news/monkey-cage/wp/2018/11/06/blame-fox-not

-facebook-for-fake-news/?noredirect=on&utm_term=
.2e59cb9e99a1.

3   Nicole Hemmer, "The Conservative War on Liberal Media Has a
Long History," *Atlantic*, January 17, 2014, https://www.the
atlantic.com/politics/archive/2014/01/the-conservative-war-on
-liberal-media-has-a-long-history/283149/.

4   Nikki Usher, "How Republicans Trick Facebook and Twitter
with Claims of Bias," *Washington Post*, August 1, 2018, https://
www.washingtonpost.com/news/posteverything/wp
/2018/08/01/how-republicans-trick-facebook-and-twitter-with
-claims-of-bias/?noredirect=on&utm_term=.77e07c5a6236.

5   "Americans' Views on the Media," Ipsos, August 7, 2018, https:
//www.ipsos.com/en-us/news-polls/americans-views-media
-2018-08-07.

6   Digby, "Trump's Muse," *Hullabaloo* (blog), April 3, 2018, https:
//digbysblog.blogspot.com/2018/04/trumps-muse.html.

7   Paul Bond, "Leslie Moonves on Donald Trump: 'It May Not Be
Good for America, but It's Damn Good for CBS,'" *Hollywood
Reporter*, February 29, 2016, https://www.hollywoodreporter
.com/news/leslie-moonves-donald-trump-may-871464.

8   James Warren, "Consolidation Is Killing the Myth of the Liberal
Media," *Vanity Fair*, November 20, 2017, https://www.vanityfair
.com/news/2017/11/consolidation-is-killing-the-myth-of-the
-liberal-media.

9   Chuck Tryon, "Debunking the Myth of the 'Liberal Media,'"
News & Observer, August 30, 2017, https://www.newsobserver
.com/opinion/op-ed/article170317567.html.

10   Anthony Salvanto, Jennifer De Pinto, Kabir Khanna, and Fred
Backus, "Americans Wary of Trump Tariffs' Impact, but Support
Plan to Aid Farmers," CBS News, July 29, 2018, https://www.cbs

news.com/news/americans-wary-of-trump-tariffs-impact-but
-support-plan-to-aid-farmers-cbs-poll/.

11   Quinnipiac University, "U.S. Voters Dislike Trump Almost 2-1,
      Quinnipiac University National Poll Finds; Media Is Important
      to Democracy, 65% Of Voters Say," news release, August 14, 2018,
      https://poll.qu.edu/search-releases/search-results/release
      -detail?ReleaseID=2561.

12   Joe Concha, "Poll: 72 Percent Say Traditional Outlets 'Report
      News They Know to Be Fake, False, or Purposely Misleading,'"
      The Hill, June 27, 2018, https://thehill.com/homenews/media
      /394352-poll-72-percent-say-traditional-outlets-report-news-they
      -know-to-be-fake-false.

13   Jeremy Barr, "Bill Shine's Massive Fox News Severance Package
      Revealed," *Hollywood Reporter,* November 23, 2018, https://www
      .hollywoodreporter.com/news/bill-shines-fox-news-severance
      -package-revealed-1163664.

14   "Lesley Stahl: Trump Admitted Mission to 'Discredit' Press,"
      CBS News, May 23, 2018, https://www.cbsnews.com/news
      /lesley-stahl-donald-trump-said-attacking-press-to-discredit
      -negative-stories/.

15   Dick Meyer, "Donald Trump's Hatred of the Press, Lies and
      Bullying Echoes Dangerous Regimes of the Past," *USA Today,*
      October 30, 2018, https://www.usatoday.com/story/opinion
      /2018/10/30/donald-trump-hatred-press-enemy-people
      -pittsburgh-shooting-synagogue-column/1817515002/.

16   Timothy Snyder, "Donald Trump and the New Dawn of
      Tyranny," *Time,* March 3, 2017, http://time.com/4690676/donald
      -trump-tyranny/.

17   Noah Smith, "Twitter's Problem Isn't the Like Button," *Bloomberg,*
      October 30, 2018, https://www.bloomberg.com/opinion/articles
      /2018-10-30/twitter-s-problem-is-bigger-than-the-like-button.

18   Adrian Shahbaz, "Freedom on the Net 2018: The Rise of Digital
      Authoritarianism" (Freedom House, October 2018), https:
      //freedomhouse.org/report/freedom-net/freedom-net-2018/rise
      -digital-authoritarianism.

19   Tim Dickinson, "How Roger Ailes Built the Fox News Fear
      Factory," *Rolling Stone*, May 25, 2011, https://www.rollingstone
      .com/politics/politics-news/how-roger-ailes-built-the-fox-news
      -fear-factory-244652/.

20   Brian Stelter, "White House pulls CNN reporter Jim Acosta's
      Pass After Contentious News Conference," CNN, November 7,
      2018, https://www.cnn.com/2018/11/07/media/trump-cnn
      -press-conference/index.html.

21   Susan Gonzalez, "Death Threats Will Not Keep April Ryan
      from Reporting the Facts, She Says," *YaleNews*, November 2, 2018,
      https://news.yale.edu/2018/11/02/death-threats-will-not-keep
      -april-ryan-reporting-facts-she-says.

22   Lauren Duca, "Donald Trump Has Been Lying to the American
      Public, and Journalists Need to Call Him Out," *Teen Vogue*, June
      1, 2018, https://www.teenvogue.com/story/thigh-high-politics
      -donald-trump-lying-journalists-need-to-call-him-out.

23   Elliot Hannon, "Today in Conservative Media: Social Media
      Bias Is the New Liberal Media Bias," *Slate*, March 08, 2018,
      https://slate.com/news-and-politics/2018/03/today-in
      -conservative-media-social-media-bias-is-the-new-liberal-media
      -bias.html.

24   Alayna Treene, "Poll: Most Conservatives Think Social
      Media Is Censoring Them," Axios, August 29, 2018, https:
      //www.axios.com/conservatives-social-media-censorship-poll
      -3a966ebb-6b44-458f-8941-40fc015a86a6.html.

25   Will Sommer, "Why a Red 'X' Is the New Symbol of
      Conservative Twitter," Daily Beast, August 10, 2018, https:

//www.thedailybeast.com/why-a-red-x-is-the-new-symbol-of
-conservative-twitter.

26 Kevin Roose and Ali Winston, "Far-Right Internet Groups
    Listen for Trump's Approval, and Often Hear It," *New York Times*,
    November 4, 2018, https://www.nytimes.com/2018/11/04/us
    /politics/far-right-internet-trump.html.

27 Andrew Restuccia, Nancy Scola, and Christopher Cadelago,
    "Behind Trump's Obsession with Social Media Suppression,"
    Politico, September 8, 2018, https://www.politico.com/story
    /2018/09/08/trump-obsession-social-media-technology-811132.

28 Declan McCullagh, "D.C. Unfriends Silicon Valley," *Reason*,
    December 2018, https://reason.com/archives/2018/11/05/dc
    -unfriends-silicon-valley.

29 Maya Kosoff, "Inside Facebook, a Conservative Backlash
    Against the Liberal 'Mobs,'" *Vanity Fair*, August 29, 2018, https:
    //www.vanityfair.com/news/2018/08/conservative-facebook
    -employees-group-liberal-culture#~0.

30 Vidya Narayanan, Vlad Barash, John Kelly, Bence Kollanyi,
    Lisa-Maria Neudert, and Philip N. Howard, "Polarization,
    Partisanship and Junk News Consumption over Social Media
    in the US" (working paper, Oxford Internet Institute, February 6,
    2018), https://comprop.oii.ox.ac.uk/research/polarization
    -partisanship-and-junk-news/.

31 Amanda Taub and Max Fisher, "Facebook Fueled Anti-Refugee
    Attacks in Germany, New Research Suggests," *New York Times*,
    August 21, 2018, https://www.nytimes.com/2018/08/21/world
    /europe/facebook-refugee-attacks-germany.html.

32 Casey Newton, "Hate Speech Is Finding a Home on Instagram,"
    The Verge, October 31, 2018, https://www.theverge.com
    /2018/10/31/18045364/instagram-hate-speech-alt-right.

33   Will Sommer, "Instagram Is the Alt-Right's New Favorite
      Haven," Daily Beast, October 20, 2018, https://www
      .thedailybeast.com/instagram-is-the-alt-rights-new-favorite
      -haven.

34   Olivia Solon, "YouTube's 'Alternative Influence Network' Breeds
      Rightwing Radicalisation, Report Finds," Guardian, September 18,
      2018, https://www.theguardian.com/media/2018/sep/18/report
      -youtubes-alternative-influence-network-breeds-rightwing
      -radicalisation.

35   Kelly Weill, "Inside YouTube's Far-Right Radicalization Factory,"
      Daily Beast, September 18, 2018, https://www.thedailybeast.com
      /inside-youtubes-far-right-radicalization-factory.

36   @animemoemoney, "A Quick History Of 4chan and the
      Rightists Who Killed It (Guest Post)," Noahpinion (blog), May 2,
      2015, http://noahpinionblog.blogspot.com/2015/05/a-quick
      -history-of-4chan-and-online.html.

37   Ben Makuch and Mack Lamoureux, "Neo-Nazis Are
      Organizing Secretive Paramilitary Training Across America,"
      VICE, November 20, 2018, https://www.vice.com/en_us/article
      /a3mexp/neo-nazis-are-organizing-secretive-paramilitary
      -training-across-america.

38   Kevin Roose, "Here Come the Fake Videos, Too," New York Times,
      March 4, 2018, https://www.nytimes.com/2018/03/04
      /technology/fake-videos-deepfakes.html.

39   Robert Chesney and Danielle Citron, "Deepfakes and the New
      Disinformation War," Foreign Affairs, January/February 2019,
      https://www.foreignaffairs.com/articles/world/2018-12-11/deep
      fakes-and-new-disinformation-war.

40   Anya Kamenetz, "Right-Wing Hate Groups Are Recruiting
      Video Gamers," NPR, November 5, 2018, https://www.npr.org

/2018/11/05/660642531/right-wing-hate-groups-are-recruiting
-video-gamers.

41   Melissa Ryan, "How the Far-Right Is Dividing Americans with
     Social Media," NowThis News, July 12, 2018, https://nowthis
     news.com/videos/politics/how-the-far-right-is-dividing
     -americans-with-social-media.

42   Mike Mariani, "Is Trump's Chaos Tornado a Move from the
     Kremlin's Playbook?" *Vanity Fair*, April 2017, https://www
     .vanityfair.com/news/2017/03/is-trumps-chaos-a-move-from
     -the-kremlins-playbook#~0.

43   Olivia Messer, "'Fox & Friends' Host: Immigrants Might Kill
     Your Children," Daily Beast, January 9, 2019, https://www.the
     dailybeast.com/fox-and-friends-host-immigrants-might-kill
     -your-children.

44   "More Than 1,800 Women Murdered by Men in One Year, New
     Study Finds," Violence Policy Center, September 18, 2018, http:
     //vpc.org/press/more-than-1800-women-murdered-by-men-in
     -one-year-new-study-finds/.

45   Eric Levenson, Samira Said, and Steve Almasy, "Man Leads
     Police to Body, Faces Murder Charge in Mollie Tibbetts Case,"
     CNN, August 22, 2018, https://www.cnn.com/2018/08/21/us
     /mollie-tibbetts-missing-iowa-student/index.html.

46   Eve Peyser, "How the Tragic Killing of Mollie Tibbetts Became a
     Right-Wing Talking Point," *VICE*, August 23, 2018, https://www
     .vice.com/en_us/article/3kymb5/how-the-tragic-killing-of
     -mollie-tibbetts-became-a-right-wing-talking-point.

47   John Binder, "Illegal Alien Charged with First Degree Murder of
     Mollie Tibbetts," Breitbart News, August 21, 2018, https://www
     .breitbart.com/politics/2018/08/21/illegal-alien-charged-with
     -first-degree-murder-of-mollie-tibbetts/.

48   Evie Fordham, "Illegal Immigrant Charged with Murder of Iowa College Student Mollie Tibbetts," Daily Caller, August 21, 2018, https://dailycaller.com/2018/08/21/illegal-immigrant -mollie-tibbetts/.

49   Aaron Colen, "Illegal Immigrant Charged with First-Degree Murder in Mollie Tibbetts' Death," The Blaze, August 21, 2018, https://www.theblaze.com/news/2018/08/21/illegal-immigrant -charged-with-first-degree-murder-in-mollie-tibbetts-death.

50   Jim Dalrymple II and Ellie Hall, "Mollie Tibbetts's Family Is Pushing Back Against Trump and His Allies After They Seized on Her Death," BuzzFeed News, August 23, 2018, https://www .buzzfeednews.com/article/jimdalrympleii/mollie-tibbetts -family-is-pushing-back-against-trump-and.

51   Rob Savillo, "Fox News' Coverage of Mollie Tibbetts' Death Spiked After It Was Linked to an Undocumented Immigrant," Media Matters for America, August 24, 2018, https://www .mediamatters.org/blog/2018/08/24/Fox-News-coverage-of -Mollie-Tibbetts-death-spiked-after-it-was-linked-to-an -undocumented-i/221103.

52   "Republicans Want to Make Mollie Tibbetts a Household Name," Axios, August 22, 2018, https://www.axios.com/2018-midterm -elections-mollie-tibbetts-republicans-8a33d987-7157-41ec-b1c3 -49544a51237c.html.

53   Shane Ryan, "The Right Wing Has Forced the National Media to Cover a Murder in Iowa Because It Involves an Undocumented Immigrant," Paste, August 22, 2018, https://www.pastemagazine .com/articles/2018/08/the-right-wing-has-forced-the-national -media-to-co.html.

54   Rob Tibbetts, "From Mollie Tibbetts' Father: Don't Distort Her Death to Advance Racist Views," Des Moines Register, September

1, 2018, https://www.desmoinesregister.com/story/opinion
/columnists/2018/09/01/mollie-tibbetts-father-common-decency
-immigration-heartless-despicable-donald-trump-jr-column
/1163131002/.

55 Alex Nowrasteh, *Criminal Immigrants in Texas: Illegal Immigrant
Conviction and Arrest Rates for Homicide, Sex Crimes, Larceny, and
Other Crimes* (Washington, DC: Cato Institute, February 26, 2018),
https://www.cato.org/publications/immigration-research
-policy-brief/criminal-immigrants-texas-illegal-immigrant.

56 Michael T. Light and Ty Miller, "Does Undocumented
Immigration Increase Violent Crime?" *Criminology* 56, no. 2 (May
2017): 370–401, https://www.ncbi.nlm.nih.gov/pmc/articles
/PMC6241529/.

CHAPTER 3

1 Abraham Lincoln, *Collected Works of Abraham Lincoln. Volume 2.*
https://quod.lib.umich.edu/l/lincoln/lincoln2/1:339?rgn=div1
;view=fulltext.

2 Office of the Director of National Intelligence, *Background to
"Assessing Russian Activities and Intentions in Recent US Elections":
The Analytic Process and Cyber Incident Attribution,* January 6, 2017,
https://www.dni.gov/files/documents/ICA_2017_01.pdf.

3 Jane Mayer, "How Russia Helped Swing the Election for Trump,"
New Yorker, October 1, 2018, https://www.newyorker.com
/magazine/2018/10/01/how-russia-helped-to-swing-the-election
-for-trump.

4 Philip Ewing, "The Russia Investigations: What You Need to
Know About Russian 'Active Measures,'" NPR, April 25, 2018,
https://www.npr.org/2018/04/25/586099619/the-russia

-investigations-what-you-need-to-know-about-russian-active
-measures.

5   Bill Whitaker, "When Russian Hackers Targeted the
U.S. Election Infrastructure," CBS News, July 17, 2018, https:
//www.cbsnews.com/news/when-russian-hackers-targeted-the
-u-s-election-infrastructure/.

6   Cynthia McFadden, William M. Arkin, and Kevin Monahan,
"Russians Penetrated U.S. Voter Systems, Top U.S. Official Says,"
NBC News, February 7, 2018, https://www.nbcnews.com
/politics/elections/russians-penetrated-u-s-voter-systems-says
-top-u-s-n845721.

7   Nancy Scola, "Massive Twitter Data Release Sheds Light on
Russia's Trump Strategy," *Politico*, October 17, 2018, https:
//www.politico.com/story/2018/10/17/twitter-foreign-influence
-operations-910005.

8   Craig Silverman, "This Analysis Shows How Viral Fake
Election News Stories Outperformed Real News on Facebook,"
BuzzFeed News, November 16, 2016, https://www.buzzfeed
news.com/article/craigsilverman/viral-fake-election-news
-outperformed-real-news-on-facebook.

9   Max Boot, "Without the Russians, Trump Wouldn't Have Won,"
Washington Post, July 24, 2018, https://www.washingtonpost
.com/opinions/without-the-russians-trump-wouldnt-have-
won/2018/07/24/f4c87894-8f6b-11e8-bcd5-9d911c784c38_story
.html?noredirect=on&utm_term=.06b7f07062b2.

10   Clint Watts, *Messing with the Enemy: Surviving in a Social Media
World of Hackers, Terrorists, Russians, and Fake News* (New York:
HarperCollins, 2018), 156.

11   Michael S. Schmidt, "Trump Invited the Russians to Hack
Clinton. Were They Listening?" *New York Times*, July 13, 2018,

https://www.nytimes.com/2018/07/13/us/politics/trump-russia
-clinton-emails.html.

12   Ellen Nakashima and Shane Harris, "How the Russians Hacked
the DNC and Passed Its Emails to WikiLeaks," *Washington Post,*
July 13, 2018, https://www.washingtonpost.com/world/national
-security/how-the-russians-hacked-the-dnc-and-passed-its
-emails-to-wikileaks/2018/07/13/af19a828-86c3-11e8-8553
-a3ce89036c78_story.html?noredirect=on&utm_term=
.48f0ce7f6ddb.

13   Mike Pompeo, "Remarks as Prepared for Delivery by Central
Intelligence Agency Director Mike Pompeo at the Center for
Strategic and International Studies," April 13, 2017, Central
Intelligence Agency, transcript, https://www.cia.gov/news
-information/speeches-testimony/2017-speeches-testimony
/pompeo-delivers-remarks-at-csis.html.

14   Eric Lipton, David E. Sanger, and Scott Shane, "The Perfect
Weapon: How Russian Cyberpower Invaded the U.S.," *New York
Times,* December 13, 2016, https://www.nytimes.com/2016/12/13
/us/politics/russia-hack-election-dnc.html.

15   Lee Ferran, Trish Turner, and Katherine Faulders, "Russia
Targeted African-American Vote, Made Instagram 'Key
Battleground' in Propaganda War: Researchers," ABC News,
December 17, 2018, https://abcnews.go.com/beta-story-container
/Politics/russia-targeted-african-american-vote-made-instagram
-key/story?id=59862038.

16   Natasha Bertrand, "DOJ Says Russian Trolls Are Interfering
Online with the Midterms," *Atlantic,* October 19, 2018, https:
//www.theatlantic.com/politics/archive/2018/10/doj-says
-russian-trolls-interfering-midterm-elections/573526/.

17   Joshua Geltzer, "Don't Be Fooled: There Was Election
Interference in 2018," Just Security, November 7, 2018,
https://www.justsecurity.org/61372/dont-fooled-was-election
-interference-2018/.

18   Mark Hertling and Molly K. McKew, "Putin's Attack on the
U.S. Is Our Pearl Harbor," *Politico,* July 16, 2018, https://www
.politico.com/magazine/story/2018/07/16/putin-russia-trump
-2016-pearl-harbor-219015.

19   Chauncey DeVega, "Intelligence Expert Malcolm Nance on
Trump Scandal: 'As Close to Benedict Arnold as We're Ever
Going to Get,'" *Salon,* March 14, 2017, https://www.salon.com
/2017/03/14/intelligence-expert-malcolm-nance-on-trump
-scandal-as-close-to-benedict-arnold-as-were-ever-going-to-get/.

20   Geoff Nunberg, "Opinion: Why the Term 'Deep State' Speaks to
Conspiracy Theorists," NPR, August 9, 2018, https://www.npr
.org/2018/08/09/633019635/opinion-why-the-term-deep-state
-speaks-to-conspiracy-theorists.

21   "Rep. Devin Nunes, Trump's Stooge, Attacks FBI," *Fresno Bee,*
January 25, 2018, https://www.fresnobee.com/opinion
/editorials/article196633904.html.

22   Jake Nevins, "Late-Night Hosts on Nunes: 'To Call Him Trump's
Lapdog Is an Insult to Dogs and Laps,'" *Guardian,* February 2,
2018, https://www.theguardian.com/culture/2018/feb/02/late
-night-hosts-on-nunes-to-call-him-trumps-lapdog-is-an-insult-to
-dogs-and-laps.

23   Manu Raju and Jeremy Herb, "House Republicans Ready
Subpoenas for James Comey, Loretta Lynch," CNN, November
16, 2018, https://www.cnn.com/2018/11/16/politics/james-comey
-loretta-lynch-subpoena/index.html.

24   Mike Allen and Jonathan Swan, "A Case Study in Trump's GOP Mind Control," Axios, July 18, 2018, https://www.axios.com /donald-trump-vladimir-putin-summit-republican-reaction -e08d9a79-82db-4268-8e31-5a4a17dac1b1.html.

25   George Will, "Trump Is No Longer the Worst Person in Government," *Washington Post,* May 9, 2018, https://www .washingtonpost.com/opinions/trump-is-no-longer-the-worst -person-in-government/2018/05/09/10e59eba-52f1-11e8-a551 -5b648abe29ef_story.html?noredirect=on&utm_term= .34c9c3431a17.

26   Zack Beauchamp, "Trump's Republican Party, Explained in One Photo," Vox, August 6, 2018, https://www.vox.com/policy-and -politics/2018/8/6/17656996/trump-republican-party-russia -rather-democrat-ohio.

27   Anthony Salvanto, Jennifer De Pinto, Fred Backus, and Kabir Khanna, "CBS News poll: Most Americans Disapprove of Trump's Handling of Putin Summit," CBS News, July 19, 2018, https://www.cbsnews.com/news/poll-trump-putin-meeting -helsinki-summit-russia-election-meddling/.

28   "Former President Barack Obama Speaks on the State of Our Democracy," Real Clear Politics, September 7, 2018, https: //www.realclearpolitics.com/video/2018/09/07/watch_live _former_president_barack_obama_speaks_on_the_state_of_our _democracy.html.

29   Brad Bannon, "Trump Effect: Republican Support for Russia Has Doubled," *The Hill,* July 18, 2018, https://thehill.com /opinion/white-house/397672-trump-effect-republican-support -for-russia-has-doubled.

30   *The Beat with Ari Melber.* Aired November 13, 2018, on MSNBC.

31   Timothy Bella, "Lindsey Graham in 2017: 'Holy Hell to Pay'
      If Sessions Is Fired. In 2018: 'When Was that? What Year?'"
      Washington Post, November 9, 2018, https://www.washington
      post.com/nation/2018/11/09/lindsey-graham-holy-hell
      -pay-if-sessions-is-fired-when-was-that-what-year
      /?noredirect=on&utm_term=.b44f6501934e.

32   Steve Benen, "Lindsey Graham Gives Democrats Odd Advice
      on Judicial Nominees," *MaddowBlog* (blog), *The Rachel Maddow
      Show*, MSNBC, September 5, 2018, http://www.msnbc.com
      /rachel-maddow-show/lindsey-graham-gives-democrats-odd
      -advice-judicial-nominees.

33   *Face the Nation*, CBS, November 11, 2018, https://www.cbsnews
      .com/news/transcript-sen-lindsey-graham-on-face-the-nation
      -november-11-2018/.

34   Rafi Schwartz, "Here's Lindsey Graham Being Confronted
      with His Raging Hypocrisy," Splinter News, November 9, 2018,
      https://splinternews.com/heres-lindsey-graham-being
      -confronted-with-his-raging-h-1830338333.

35   Charles P. Pierce, "There Is No More Loathsome Creature
      Walking Our Political Landscape Than Mitch McConnell,"
      Esquire, January 29, 2019, https://www.esquire.com/news
      -politics/politics/a25956710/mitch-mcconnell-op-ed-voting-bill
      -democrats/.

36   Kurt Andersen, "How America Lost Its Mind," *Atlantic*,
      September 2017, https://www.theatlantic.com/magazine
      /archive/2017/09/how-america-lost-its-mind/534231/.

CHAPTER 4

1   John Hinderaker, "Why Do Democrats Hate America?" *Power Line*, July 4, 2018, https://www.powerlineblog.com./archives /2018/07/why-do-democrats-hate-america.php

2   John Schaar, "What is Patriotism?" *Nation,* July 15, 1991, https://www.thenation.com/article/what-patriotism/.

3   Sydney J. Harris, *Strictly Personal* (Chicago: H. Regnery, 1953), 228.

4   Jen Sorensen, "Nationalism Isn't Patriotism," The Nib, November 15, 2017, https://thenib.com/nationalism-isn-t-patriotism.

5   George Orwell, "Notes on Nationalism," May 1945, https://www.orwellfoundation.com/the-orwell-foundation/orwell /essays-and-other-works/notes-on-nationalism/.

6   Theodore Roosevelt, "Lincoln and Free Speech," *Metropolitan* 47, no. 6 (May 1918): 7–8, https://babel.hathitrust.org/cgi/pt?id=uva .x030708290;view=1up;seq=5.

7   Nathaniel Rakich and Dhrumil Mehta, "We're Divided on Patriotism Too," FiveThirtyEight, July 6, 2018, https://fivethirty eight.com/features/were-divided-on-patriotism-too/.

8   Steve Wyche, "Colin Kaepernick Explains Why He Sat During National Anthem," NFL Media, August 27, 2016, http://www.nfl .com/news/story/0ap3000000691077/article/colin-kaepernick -explains-why-he-sat-during-national-anthem.

9   Megan Garber, "They Took a Knee," *Atlantic,* September 24, 2017, https://www.theatlantic.com/entertainment/archive/2017/09 /why-the-nfl-is-protesting/540927/.

10 Mychal Denzel Smith, "Colin Kaepernick's Protest Might Be Unpatriotic. And That's Just Fine," *Guardian,* September 12, 2018, https://www.theguardian.com/commentisfree/2018/sep/12 /colin-kaepernicks-protest-unpatriotic-justice.

11   Simon McCormack, "New Video of Tamir Rice Shooting Shows Police Arresting Sister, Delaying First Aid," HuffPost, December 6, 2017, https://www.huffingtonpost.com/2015/01/08/new-video -tamir-rice_n_6436040.html.

12   Cory Shaffer, "Cleveland Police Officer Shoots 12-Year-Old Boy Carrying BB Gun," Cleveland.com, November 22, 2014, https: //www.cleveland.com/metro/index.ssf/2014/11/cleveland _police_officer_shoot_6.html.

13   Steven W. Thrasher, "Tamir Rice Was Killed by White America's Irrational Fear of Black Boys," *Guardian*, December 29, 2015, https://www.theguardian.com/commentisfree/2015/dec/29 /tamir-rice-killed-by-white-americas-irrational-fear-black-boys.

14   Jelani Cobb, "Tamir Rice and America's Tragedy," *New Yorker*, December 29, 2015, https://www.newyorker.com/news/daily -comment/tamir-rice-and-americas-tragedy.

15   Jamilah Lemieux, "Sandra Bland: A Black Woman's Life Finally Matters," Gawker, July 28, 2015, https://gawker.com/sandra -bland-and-why-we-can-no-longer-look-away-1720634864.

16   Shirley Chisholm, *Unbought and Unbossed* (Boston: Houghton Mifflin, 1970), 183.

17   Kathryn Casteel, "How Do Americans Feel About the NFL Protests? It Depends on How You Ask," FiveThirtyEight, October 9, 2017, https://fivethirtyeight.com/features/how-do -americans-feel-about-the-nfl-protests-it-depends-on-how-you -ask/.

18   Chad Williams, "NFL Tells Players Patriotism Is More Important Than Protest—Here's Why That Didn't Work During WWI," *The Conversation*, May 29, 2018, https://theconversation .com/nfl-tells-players-patriotism-is-more-important-than-protest -heres-why-that-didnt-work-during-wwi-97360.

19   Martenzie Johnson, "Let's Take the National Anthem Literally, and the Songwriter at His Word," The Undefeated, August 30, 2016, https://theundefeated.com/features/lets-take-the-national -anthem-literally-and-the-songwriter-at-his-word/.

20   36 U.S.C. § 171 (1994), https://www.govinfo.gov/content/pkg/US CODE-1994-title36/html/USCODE-1994-title36-chap10.htm.

21   John Pavlovitz, "These Protests Have Never Been About a Flag, an Anthem, or the Military," *John Pavlovitz* (blog), September 26, 2017, https://johnpavlovitz.com/2017/09/26/protests-arent-flag -anthem-military-know/.

22   Ana Blinder, "An Insider's Account of the NFL Players' Take-a-Knee Movement," *Speak Freely* (blog), ACLU, September 9, 2018, https://www.aclu.org/blog/racial-justice/insiders-account-nfl -players-take-knee-movement.

23   Nate Boyer, "Ex-Green Beret Nate Boyer Writes Open Letter to Trump, Kaepernick, NFL and America," ESPN, October 13, 2017, http://www.espn.com/nfl/story/_/id/21003968/nfl-2017 -ex-green-beret-nate-boyer-writes-open-letter-president-donald -trump-colin-kaepernick-nfl-united-states-america.

24   Jonathan Evans, "People Are Already Burning Their Nikes in Response to the Colin Kaepernick Ad," *Esquire,* September 4, 2018, https://www.esquire.com/style/mens-fashion/a22969808 /colin-kaepernick-nike-ad-burning-sneakers-response/.

25   Pierre Thomas and Jack Date, "Russian Internet Trolls Pushing #TakeAKnee, #BoycottNFL to Sow Discord in US: Senator," ABC News, September 27, 2017, https://abcnews.go.com/Politics /russian-internet-trolls-calling-takeaknee-boycottnf-sow -discord/story?id=50132807.

26   NowThis (@nowthisnews), "'I can think of nothing more American.'—Beto O'Rourke—the man taking on Ted Cruz—

brilliantly explains why NFL players kneeling during the anthem is not . . . ," Twitter, August 21, 2018, https://twitter.com /nowthisnews/status/1032017750829531142/video/1

27 Tim Lee, "Ted Cruz for Senate Releases Digital Ad 'Stand for the Anthem,'" TedCruz.org, August 27, 2018, https://www.tedcruz .org/press-releases/ted-cruz-for-senate-releases-digital-ad-stand -for-the-anthem/.

28 Nicole Gaouette, "Trump's Military Insults Are Piling Up," CNN, November 19, 2018, https://www.cnn.com/2018/11/19 /politics/trump-military-insults-compliments/index.html.

29 Catherine Lucey, Zeke Miller, and Jonathan Lemire, "Read the Transcript of AP's Interview with President Trump," Associated Press, October 17, 2018, https://apnews.com/ce719c7d666 4400cb6b720ba84af2bc2.

30 Nikki Wentling, "Congress Approves Measure to Hold VA Accountable for GI Bill Payments," *Stars and Stripes*, December 20, 2018, https://www.stripes.com/news/congress-approves -measure-to-hold-va-accountable-for-gi-bill-payments-1.561506.

31 Erick Erickson, "If Obama Had Done This," The Resurgent, June 12, 2018, https://www.themaven.net/theresurgent/erick -erickson/if-obama-had-done-this--ybJnNdkAU2G0Y50XJqQsg/.

32 Cynthia Lee, "It Looks Like Another Black Man with a Gun Was Killed by Police After Trying to Help," *Slate,* November 29, 2018, https://slate.com/news-and-politics/2018/11/ej-bradford-jemel -roberson-police-shootings-good-guy-with-gun.html.

CHAPTER 5

1 Dalia Fahmy, "Americans Are Far More Religious than Adults in Other Wealthy Nations," Pew Research Center, July 31, 2018,

http://www.pewresearch.org/fact-tank/2018/07/31/americans
-are-far-more-religious-than-adults-in-other-wealthy-nations/.

2   Frank Newport, "Three-Quarters of Americans Identify as
    Christian," Gallup News, December 24, 2014, https://news
    .gallup.com/poll/180347/three-quarters-americans-identify
    -christian.aspx.

3   David Brody, "Exclusive: Michele Bachmann: This Will Be 'Last
    Election' If Hillary Wins Presidency," CBN News, September 1,
    2016, https://www1.cbn.com/thebrodyfile/archive/2016/09/01
    /only-on-the-brody-file-michele-bachmann-says-this-will-be
    -last-election-if-hillary-wins-presidency.

4   "David Barton," Southern Poverty Law Center, accessed January
    9, 2019, https://www.splcenter.org/fighting-hate/extremist-files
    /individual/david-barton.

5   Steven K. Green, "Was America Founded as a Christian Nation?"
    CNN, July 4, 2015, https://www.cnn.com/2015/07/02/living
    /america-christian-nation/index.html.

6   George Lakoff, "Our Moral Values," *Nation*, November 18, 2004,
    https://www.thenation.com/article/our-moral-values/.

7   Stephen M. Walt, "The Myth of American Exceptionalism,"
    Foreign Policy, October 11, 2011, https://foreignpolicy.com
    /2011/10/11/the-myth-of-american-exceptionalism/.

8   John F. Kennedy, "Inaugural Address," January 20, 1961, JFK
    Library, transcript, https://www.jfklibrary.org/learn/about-jfk
    /historic-speeches/inaugural-address.

9   Jay Bookman, "Opinion: GOP Explicitly Selling Itself as the
    Christian Party," *Atlanta Journal-Constitution*, May 29, 2018,
    https://www.ajc.com/news/opinion/opinion-gop-explicitly
    -selling-itself-the-christian-party/UwDIaTdnOjJMShVCaJsE2J/.

10 Elizabeth Cady Stanton, *The Woman's Bible: A Classic Feminist Perspective* (Mineola, NY: Dover, 2002), 216.

11 "The Propaganda of Deception," United States Holocaust Memorial Museum, accessed January 9, 2019, https://www.ushmm.org/propaganda/themes/deceiving-the-public/.

12 Julie Zauzmer and Keith McMillan, "Sessions Cites Bible Passage Used to Defend Slavery in Defense of Separating Immigrant Families," *Washington Post*, June 15, 2018, https://www.washingtonpost.com/news/acts-of-faith/wp/2018/06/14/jeff-sessions-points-to-the-bible-in-defense-of-separating-immigrant-families/?noredirect=on&utm_term=.9b70caff8d36.

13 "In the Freezer: Abusive Conditions for Women and Children in US Immigration Holding Cells," Human Rights Watch, February 28, 2018, https://www.hrw.org/report/2018/02/28/freezer/abusive-conditions-women-and-children-us-immigration-holding-cells#.

14 Jessica Durham and Sean Billings, "Jesuit Priest Responds to Jeff Sessions's Use of Bible to Defend Separating Immigrant Families: 'Read All the Verses,'" *Newsweek*, June 20, 2018, https://www.newsweek.com/jesuit-priest-jeff-sessions-romans-13-bible-immigrant-families-984735.

15 Christian Century staff, Religion News Service staff, and the Christian Science Monitor staff, "Churches Rebuke Jeff Sessions on Immigration Rules," *Christian Century*, June 14, 2018, https://www.christiancentury.org/article/news/churches-rebuke-jeff-sessions-immigration-rules.

16 Michael Burke, "United Methodist Church Dismisses Complaint from Members Against Jeff Sessions: Report," *The Hill*, August 8, 2018, https://thehill.com/homenews

/administration/400874-united-methodist-church-dismisses
-complaint-from-members-against-jeff.

17   Sarah McCammon, "Evangelicals Push Back on Sessions' Use of
     Bible Passage to Defend Immigration Policy," NPR, June 15, 2018,
     https://www.npr.org/2018/06/15/620471106/evangelicals-push
     -back-on-sessions-use-of-bible-passage-to-defend-immigrationpo.

18   Rosemary Agonito, *Hypocrisy, Inc.: How the Religious Right
     Fabricates Christian Values and Undermines Democracy* (self-pub.,
     Create Space, 2012), Chapter 1, Kindle.

19   David S. Glosser, "Stephen Miller Is an Immigration Hypocrite.
     I Know Because I'm His Uncle," *Politico*, August 13, 2018, https:
     //www.politico.com/magazine/story/2018/08/13/stephen-miller
     -is-an-immigration-hypocrite-i-know-because-im-his-uncle
     -219351.

20   Matthew Soerens, "Sorry Jeff Sessions, the Bible Doesn't Justify
     Terrorizing Parents & Children on the Border," *USA Today*, June
     18, 2018, https://www.usatoday.com/story/opinion/2018/06/18
     /jeff-sessions-zero-tolerance-separating-families-romans-13
     -bible-column/709762002/.

21   ACLU, "ACLU Border Rights Center Statement on Child's Death
     in Border Patrol Custody," press release, December 13, 2018,
     https://www.aclusandiego.org/aclu-border-rights-center
     -statement-on-childs-death-in-border-patrol-custody/.

22   Lukas Mikelionis, "Dems, Progressives Quick to Politicize
     Death of Migrant Girl in Border Patrol Custody," Fox News,
     December 14, 2018, https://www.foxnews.com/politics/2020
     -dem-candidates-progressives-weaponize-death-of-dehydrated
     -migrant-girl-in-border-patrol-custody.

23   Joel Baden, "Franklin Graham Said Immigration Is 'Not a Bible
     Issue.' Here's What the Bible Says," *Washington Post*, February 10,

2017, https://www.washingtonpost.com/news/acts-of-faith/wp
/2017/02/10/franklin-graham-said-immigration-is-not-a-bible
-issue-heres-what-the-bible-says/?noredirect=on&utm_term=
.0a1bb0ea874b.

24   Daniel Darling, "Christians Should See in the Migrant Caravan
     the Bible's Call to Honor the Dignity of All Humanity,"
     Washington Post, November 2, 2018, https://www
     .washingtonpost.com/religion/2018/11/02/christians-should
     -see-migrant-caravan-bibles-call-honor-dignity-all-humanity
     /?noredirect=on&utm_term=.4cbe4cf16731.

25   Elizabeth Podrebarac Sciupac and Gregory A. Smith, "How
     Religious Groups Voted in the Midterm Elections," Pew
     Research Center, November 7, 2018, http://www.pewresearch
     .org/fact-tank/2018/11/07/how-religious-groups-voted-in-the
     -midterm-elections/.

26   Tara Isabella Burton, "The Bible Says to Welcome Immigrants.
     So Why Don't White Evangelicals?" Vox, October 30, 2018,
     https://www.vox.com/2018/10/30/18035336/white-evangelicals
     -immigration-nationalism-christianity-refugee-honduras-migrant.

27   Robert P. Jones, *The End of White Christian America* (New York:
     Simon & Schuster, 2016), 248.

28   David Smith, "Love of Trump Covers a Multitude of Sins for
     Christian Conservatives," *Guardian,* September 22, 2018, https:
     //www.theguardian.com/us-news/2018/sep/21/christian
     -conservatives-trump-values-voters.

29   Stephanie McCrummen, "God, Trump and the Meaning of
     Morality," *Washington Post,* July 21, 2018, https://www
     .washingtonpost.com/news/national/wp/2018/07/21/feature
     /god-trump-and-the-meaning-of-morality/?noredirect
     =on&utm_term=.eba5711ea243.

30   Kyle Mantyla, "Alex Jones: Trump Has Privately Told Me Many Times 'How Much He Loves God,'" Right Wing Watch, December 4, 2018, http://www.rightwingwatch.org/post/alex-jones-trump-has-privately-told-me-many-times-how-much-he-loves-god/.

31   Rose White, "Why Are Christians Republican?" Medium, November 9, 2016, https://medium.com/@rosekellywhite/why-are-christians-republican-15a910a0d50a.

32   Isha Aran, "Extreme Homophobe Mike Pence Doesn't Seem to Get Why a Gay Person Won't Talk to Him," Splinter News, February 7, 2018, https://splinternews.com/extreme-homophobe-mike-pence-doesnt-seem-to-get-why-a-g-1822806959.

33   Christopher Brito, "Omarosa: We'd Be 'Begging For Trump Back' If Mike Pence Were President," CBS News, February 13, 2018, https://www.cbsnews.com/news/omarosa-donald-trump-mike-pence-president-celebrity-big-brother/.

34   John Aravosis, "Trump VP Pick Mike Pence: Cut AIDS Funding, Use It to 'Cure' Gays Instead," *AmericaBlog* (blog), July 15, 2016, http://elections.americablog.com/2016/07/wooing-gays-trump-picks-rabid-homophobe-mike-pence-vp.html.

35   Jeremy Scahill, "Mike Pence Will Be the Most Powerful Christian Supremacist in U.S. History," The Intercept, November 15, 2016, https://theintercept.com/2016/11/15/mike-pence-will-be-the-most-powerful-christian-supremacist-in-us-history/.

36   John Fea, "Mike Pence Tells Pastors to 'Share the Good News of Jesus Christ,'" *The Way of Improvement* (blog), May 26, 2018, https://thewayofimprovement.com/2018/05/26/mike-pence-tells-pastors-to-share-the-good-news-of-jesus-christ/.

37 Melissa McEwan, "On Mike Pence's Destructive Ambition," *Shakesville* (blog), May 16, 2018, http://www.shakesville.com /2018/05/on-mike-pences-destructive-ambition.html.

38 Kathy Frankovic, "Moral Judgments Often Split Along Party Lines," YouGov, March 19, 2018, https://today.yougov .com/topics/philosophy/articles-reports/2018/03/19/moral -judgments-often-split-along-party-lines.

39 Jason Sattler, "Stormy Daniels and Donald Trump, Brought to You by Mike Pence and the Religious Right," *USA Today*, March 26, 2018, https://www.usatoday.com/story/opinion/2018/03/26 /stormy-daniels-donald-trump-thanks-mike-pence-evangelicals -column/457212002/.

40 Jeff Sharlet, "The Odd Couple: While Trump Openly Cheated on Ex-Wife, Pence Called for Criminalizing Adultery," interview by Amy Goodman, *Democracy Now!*, July 21, 2016, https://www .democracynow.org/2016/7/21/reporter_who_unearthed_pence _radio_tapes.

41 Michael D'Antonio, interview by Christiane Amanpour, *Amanpour*, CNN, September 4, 2018, http://transcripts.cnn.com /TRANSCRIPTS/1809/04/ampr.01.html.

42 Christopher Stroop, "Authoritarian Christianity, or, What Franklin Graham Really Means When He Equates Progressivism with Godlessness," *Not Your Mission Field* (blog), May 30, 2018, https://chrisstroop.com/2018/05/30/authoritarian -christianity-or-what-franklin-graham-really-means-when-he -equates-progressivism-with-godlessness/.

43 Chauncey DeVega, "Have Christian Nationalists Staged a 'Soft Coup,' with Trump as Their Figurehead?" *Salon*, April 5, 2018, https://www.salon.com/2018/04/05/have-christian-nationalists -staged-a-soft-coup-with-trump-as-their-figurehead/.

44   Sean McElwee, "It's Time to Abolish ICE," *Nation,* March 9, 2018, https://www.thenation.com/article/its-time-to-abolish-ice/.

45   Tim Rymel, "The Christian Right's Abdication of Moral Guidance," HuffPost, January 9, 2018, https://www.huffington post.com/entry/the-christian-rights-abdication-of-moral -guidance_us_5a552ff4e4b0baa6abf1621f.

CHAPTER 6

1   Caroline Reilly, "'Shout Your Abortion' Is Changing the Conversation," *Bitch,* November 1, 2018, https://www.bitch media.org/article/shout-your-abortion-book.

2   Madeleine Davies, "Amelia Bonow Explains How #ShoutYourAbortion 'Just Kicked the Patriarchy in the Dick,'" Jezebel, September 25, 2015, https://jezebel.com/amelia-bonow -explains-how-shoutyourabortion-just-kicke-1732379155.

3   "Public Opinion on Abortion," Pew Research Center, October 15, 2018, http://www.pewforum.org/fact-sheet/public-opinion-on -abortion/.

4   Ilyse Hogue, "NARAL President Ilyse Hogue: The War Against Abortion Is a War Against Female Autonomy," interview by Dawn Porter, *Lenny Letter,* March 2, 2016, https://www.lenny letter.com/story/naral-president-ilyse-hogue-the-war-against -abortion-is-a-war-against-female-autonomy.

5   Morgan Brinlee, "How Americans United for Life Has Been Pushing TRAP Laws Since Before Roe v. Wade," Bustle, January 22, 2018, https://www.bustle.com/p/how-americans-united -for-life-has-been-pushing-trap-laws-since-before-roe-v-wade -7968168.

6   Bridget Freihart, "Young Feminist: TRAP-ped: Americans
     United for Life and the Co-Optation of Women's Health,"
     National Women's Health Network, May 5, 2016, https://www
     .nwhn.org/young-feminist-trap-ped-americans-united-life-co
     -optation-womens-health/.

7   "Personhood," Rewire.News, last updated November 7, 2018,
     https://rewire.news/legislative-tracker/law-topic/personhood/.

8   Linda C. Fentiman, "Women as Incubators: How US Law
     Dehumanizes Pregnant Women," Broadly, April 12, 2017,
     https://broadly.vice.com/en_us/article/d3gpwz/women
     -incubators-us-law-criminalizes-pregnant-women.

9   Carmen Rios, "Daring to Remember: Tell Us Your Story of Life
     Before Roe," *Ms.*, July 2, 2018, http://msmagazine.com/blog
     /2018/07/02/daring-remember-tell-us-story-life-roe/.

10   Katha Pollitt, *Pro: Reclaiming Abortion Rights* (New York: Picador,
     2014), 15.

11   Jessica Ravitz, "The Surprising History of Abortion in the
     United States," CNN, June 27, 2016, https://www.cnn.com
     /2016/06/23/health/abortion-history-in-united-states/index
     .html.

12   "History of Abortion," National Abortion Federation, accessed
     January 9, 2019, https://prochoice.org/education-and-advocacy
     /about-abortion/history-of-abortion/.

13   bell hooks, *Feminism Is for Everybody: Passionate Politics* (London:
     Pluto Press, 2000), 6.

14   Laurie Penny, "If Men Got Pregnant, Abortion Would Be Legal
     Everywhere," *New Statesman*, December 4, 2015, https://www
     .newstatesman.com/politics/feminism/2015/12/if-men-got
     -pregnant-abortion-would-be-legal-everywhere.

15   Jeanne Mancini, "We Won't Stop Marching," March for Life, January 22, 2018, https://marchforlife.org/author/j-monahan/.

16   Abby Johnson (website), accessed January 9, 2019, www.abby johnson.org/.

17   Ed Kilgore, "Why Anti-Abortion Activists Are Obsessed with Late-Term Abortion Bans," *The Cut,* October 3, 2017, https: //www.thecut.com/2017/10/late-term-abortion-ban-pro-life -activists.html.

18   Laura Kacere, "The Truth Behind Late-Term Abortions," Everyday Feminism, June 6, 2014, https://everydayfeminism .com/2014/06/truth-late-term-abortions/.

19   Laura Kasinof, "The Secret Evangelicals at Planned Parenthood," *Marie Claire,* May 31, 2017, https://www.marieclaire.com/politics /a27333/secret-evangelical-christians-at-planned-parenthood/.

20   Stephen Altrogge, "Praying Psalms of Destruction Against Planned Parenthood," *The Blazing Center* (blog), August 23, 2015, https://theblazingcenter.com/2015/08/praying-psalms-of -destruction-against-planned-parenthood.html.

21   Paige Williams, "Sarah Huckabee Sanders, Trump's Battering Ram," *New Yorker,* September 24, 2018, https://www.newyorker .com/magazine/2018/09/24/sarah-huckabee-sanders-trumps -battering-ram.

22   Ed Mazza, "Michelle Wolf Absolutely Nails Pro-Life Hypocrisy: They 'Do Not Care About Life,'" HuffPost, July 10, 2018, https: //www.huffingtonpost.com/entry/michelle-wolf-pro-life-netflix _us_5b42c328e4b09e4a8b2e77d8.

23   Alex Palombo, "Pro-Life vs. Pro-Birth," HuffPost, July 11, 2013, https://www.huffingtonpost.com/alex-palombo/pro-life-vs-pro -birth_b_3579527.html.

24   Eric Sammons, "Why I'm Through Being 'Pro-Life,'"
      CatholicVote.org, July 9, 2018, https://catholicvote.org/why-im
      -through-being-pro-life/.

25   Madeleine Aggeler, "This Man's Question to People Who Are
      Anti-Abortion Challenges One of Their Main Arguments,"
      Bustle, October 23, 2017, https://www.bustle.com/p/this-mans
      -question-to-people-who-are-anti-abortion-challenges-one-of
      -their-main-arguments-2975437.

26   Paul Rosenberg, "The Twitter Thought Experiment That
      Exposes 'Pro-Life' Hypocrisy," *Salon*, October 22, 2017, https:
      //www.salon.com/2017/10/22/the-twitter-thought-experiment
      -that-exposes-pro-life-hypocrisy/.

27   William Grimes, "Philippa Foot, Renowned Philosopher, Dies at
      90," *New York Times*, October 9, 2010, https://www.nytimes.com
      /2010/10/10/us/10foot.html.

28   Eric Rakowski, introduction to *The Trolley Problem Mysteries*
      (New York: Oxford University Press, 2016), introduction.

29   Frances Myrna Kamm, *The Trolley Problem Mysteries* (New York:
      Oxford University Press, 2016), 12.

30   Berny Belvedere, "Here's an Honest Answer to That Dumb
      Twitter Rant on Abortion," *Weekly Standard*, October 17, 2017,
      https://www.weeklystandard.com/berny-belvedere/heres-an
      -honest-answer-to-that-dumb-twitter-rant-on-abortion.

31   Ben Shapiro, "This Pro-Abortion Fanatic Presented a Thought
      Experiment 'DESTROYING' Pro-Lifers. Here Are 4 Reasons He
      Fails Dramatically," Daily Wire, October 17, 2017, https://www
      .dailywire.com/news/22360/pro-abortion-fanatic-presented
      -thought-experiment-ben-shapiro.

32   Charlie Rae, "Patrick Tomlinson v. Ben Shapiro, Men Attempt
      Abortion Logic," Fifth Column News, October 24, 2017, https:

//thefifthcolumnnews.com/2017/10/patrick-tomlinson-v-ben
-shapiro-abortion/.

33   Karissa Miller, "Why We Lose the Abortion Debate" Medium,
      October 23, 2017, https://medium.com/@karissakmiller/why-we
      -lose-the-abortion-debate-957df66cc39.

34   Anastasia Somoza, "My Health Care Is at Stake in
      November," Medium, October 25, 2018, https://medium.com
      /@TheDemocrats/my-health-care-is-at-stake-in-november
      -c5dcae931e0c.

35   Andrew Desiderio, "Secret Pro-Life Meeting with Mike Pence
      Killed Obamacare Fix—for Now," Daily Beast, January 9, 2018,
      https://www.thedailybeast.com/secret-pro-life-meeting-with
      -mike-pence-killed-obamacare-fixfor-now.

CHAPTER 7

1   State of Connecticut Office of the Child Advocate, *Shooting at
      Sandy Hook Elementary School*, November 21, 2014, https://www
      .ct.gov/oca/lib/oca/sandyhook11212014.pdf.

2   Larry Buchanan, Josh Keller, Richard A. Oppel, Jr., and Daniel
      Victor, "How They Got Their Guns," *New York Times*, February
      16, 2018, https://www.nytimes.com/interactive/2015/10/03/us
      /how-mass-shooters-got-their-guns.html.

3   Dave Altimari, "Sandy Hook Shooter Adam Lanza's
      Spreadsheet Detailing Centuries of Mass Violence Served as
      a Road Map to Murder," *Hartford Courant*, December 9, 2018,
      https://www.courant.com/news/connecticut/hc-news-sandy
      -hook-lanza-spreadsheet-20181205-story.html.

4   "Key Gun Violence Statistics," Brady Campaign to Prevent Gun
      Violence, accessed January 9, 2019, http://www.brady
      campaign.org/key-gun-violence-statistics.

5	Global Burden of Disease 2016 Injury Collaborators, "Global Mortality from Firearms, 1990–2016," *JAMA* 320, no. 8 (2018): 792–814, doi:10.1001/jama.2018.10060.

6	Lois Beckett, "The Gun Numbers: Just 3% of American Adults Own a Collective 133m Firearms," *Guardian*, November 15, 2017, https://www.theguardian.com/us-news/2017/nov/15/the-gun-numbers-just-3-of-american-adults-own-a-collective-133m-firearms.

7	Sandee LaMotte, "US Leads the World in Child Gun Deaths," CNN, December 20, 2018, https://www.cnn.com/2018/12/20/health/child-gun-deaths-rising/index.html.

8	Asma Khalid, "NPR Poll: After Parkland, Number of Americans Who Want Gun Restrictions Grows," NPR, March 2, 2018, https://www.npr.org/2018/03/02/589849342/npr-poll-after-parkland-number-of-americans-who-want-gun-restrictions-grows.

9	Ryan Sit, "Here's Why the NRA Is So Powerful and Why Gun Control Advocates Have Reason for Hope," *Newsweek*, February 22, 2018, https://www.newsweek.com/nra-gun-control-parkland-florida-school-shooting-campaign-donations-813940.

10	Natasha Lennard, "The First Step Act Is Not Sweeping Criminal Justice Reform—and the Risk Is That It Becomes the Only Step," The Intercept, December 19, 2018, https://theintercept.com/2018/12/19/first-step-act-criminal-justice-reform-bill/.

11	Tammy Duckworth, "I'm a Combat Veteran. We Cannot Allow Our Country to Be Turned Into a War Zone," *Washington Post*, December 19, 2018, https://www.washingtonpost.com/opinions/im-a-combat-veteran-we-cannot-allow-our-country-to-be-turned-into-a-war-zone/2018/12/19/c4dee01e-03b5-11e9-b5df-5d3874f1ac36_story.html?noredirect=on&utm_term=.6de78a5430c8.

12   Michael Hiltzik, "'Thoughts and prayers' and Fistfuls of NRA Money: Why America Can't Control Guns (a Grim Update)," *Los Angeles Times*, February 15, 2018, https://www.latimes.com /business/hiltzik/la-fi-hiltzik-nra-politicians-20180215-story.html.

13   *CNN Town Hall*, "Gun Policy in America," CNN, February 21, 2018.

14   Richard Wolffe, "Marco Rubio Almost Got Away with His Routine. Then He Met Cameron Kasky," *Guardian*, February 22, 2018, https://www.theguardian.com/us-news/comment isfree/2018/feb/21/marco-rubio-cameron-kasky-cnn-town-hall -florida-gun-control.

15   Sharyn Alfonsi, "Students Calling for Change After the Parkland Shooting," *60 Minutes*, CBS, March 18, 2018, https: //www.cbsnews.com/news/parkland-shooting-students -calling-for-change-60-minutes-interview/.

16   Terry Gross, "A Trauma Surgeon Who Survived Gun Violence Is Taking on the NRA," NPR, November 28, 2018, https://www .npr.org/sections/health-shots/2018/11/28/671519701/this -trauma-surgeon-survived-gun-violence-now-hes-taking-on-the -nra.

17   Daniel Desrochers, "McConnell Says There Isn't Much Federal Government Can Do About School Shootings," *Lexington Herald-Leader*, July 3, 2018, https://www.kentucky.com/news/politics -government/article214224494.html.

18   John Paul Stevens, "John Paul Stevens: Repeal the Second Amendment," *New York Times*, March 27, 2018, https://www.ny times.com/2018/03/27/opinion/john-paul-stevens-repeal-second -amendment.html.

19   Everytown for Gun Safety, *Not Your Grandparents' NRA: How the Leadership of the NRA Puts Americans at Risk*, April 2014, https: //everytownresearch.org/reports/not-your-grandparents-nra/.

20   David Roberts, "The Caravan 'Invasion' and America's
      Epistemic Crisis," Vox, November 2, 2018, https://www.vox
      .com/policy-and-politics/2018/11/1/18041710/migrant-caravan
      -america-trump-epistemic-crisis-democracy.

CHAPTER 8

1   Coretta Scott King, Coretta: My Life, My Love, My Legacy (New
      York: Henry Holt, 2017), 178.

2   Amy Plitt and Tanay Warerkar, "Wilbur Ross's Lavish
      Billionaires' Row Penthouse Sells at a Loss for $15.95M," Curbed,
      October 26, 2017, https://ny.curbed.com/2017/3/3/14801958
      /wilbur-rosss-billionaires-row-penthouse-sold/comment
      /418049799.

3   Simone Foxman and Sonali Basak, "It's Billionaires at the Gate as
      Ultra-Rich Muscle In on Private Equity," Bloomberg, June 11, 2018,
      https://www.bloomberg.com/news/articles/2018-06-11/it-s
      -billionaires-at-the-gate-as-ultra-rich-muscle-in-on-private-equity.

4   Dan Alexander, "New Details About Wilbur Ross' Business
      Point to Pattern of Grifting," Forbes, August 7, 2018, https:
      //www.forbes.com/sites/danalexander/2018/08/06/new-details
      -about-wilbur-rosss-businesses-point-to-pattern-of-grifting
      /#616d15191c33.

5   Tim Dickinson, "Inside the Trump Administration's Census
      Scam," Rolling Stone, December 13, 2018, https://www.rolling
      stone.com/politics/politics-features/2020-census-citizenship
      -question-wilbur-ross-767078/.

6   Ananya Bhattacharya, "Isha Ambani Wedding Festivities
      in Udaipur: Date, Venue And Exclusive Details," India Today,
      December 9, 2018, https://www.indiatoday.in/lifestyle/celebrity

/story/isha-ambani-wedding-udaipur-exclusive-details
-1405161-2018-12-08.

7   "Udaipur Turns into Davos as Fortune 500 CEOs, Hillary
      Clinton Arrive for Isha Ambani's Wedding," News18, December
      9, 2018, https://www.news18.com/news/india/hillary-clinton
      -lakshmi-mittal-sachin-tendulkar-arrive-for-isha-ambanis-pre
      -wedding-celebration-in-udaipur-1964697.html.

8   John Smith, *The Generall Historie of Virginia, New England and the
      Summer Isles* (Bedford, MA: Applewood Books, 2006), 1: 232.

9   Justin Fox, "It's Beginning to Look a Lot Like the Gilded Age,"
      Bloomberg, February 7, 2018, https://www.bloomberg.com
      /opinion/articles/2018-02-07/it-s-beginning-to-look-a-lot-like
      -the-gilded-age.

10   Chapo Trap House, Felix Biederman, Matt Christman, Brendan
      James, Will Menaker, Virgil Texas, *The Chapo Guide to Revolution:
      A Manifesto Against Logic, Facts, and Reason* (New York:
      Touchstone, 2018), 4.

11   Jonathan Chait, "Why the Bernie Movement Must Crush Beto
      O'Rourke," *New York Magazine,* December 28, 2018, http://nymag
      .com/intelligencer/2018/12/bernie-sanders-beto-orourke-feud
      -2020-campaign-democratic.html.

12   Robert J. Shapiro, "Does Science Prove That the Modern
      GOP Favors the Rich?" *FixGov* (blog), Brookings Institution,
      December 6, 2017, https://www.brookings.edu/blog/fixgov
      /2017/12/06/does-science-prove-that-the-modern-gop-favors
      -the-rich/.

13   Eugene Scott, "To Some Conservatives, 'Elite' Is Just a Word
      That Means 'Them,'" *Washington Post,* May 1, 2018, https://www
      .washingtonpost.com/news/the-fix/wp/2018/05/01/to-some
      -conservatives-elite-is-just-a-word-that-means-them/?noredirect
      =on&utm_term=.033ba88e0ac5.

14   Paul Krugman, "Stop Calling Trump a Populist," *New York Times*, August 2, 2018, https://www.nytimes.com/2018/08/02/opinion/stop-calling-trump-a-populist.html.

15   Elizabeth Williamson, "Meet the Schlapps, Washington's Trump-Era 'It Couple,'" *New York Times*, April 30, 2018, https://www.nytimes.com/2018/04/30/us/politics/schlapp-trump.html?smid=tw-share.

16   Bob Bryan, "One of Republicans' Biggest Promises About Their Tax Law Is Coming Apart at the Seams," Business Insider, October 16, 2018, https://www.businessinsider.com/gop-trump-tax-law-budget-deficit-debt-2018-10.

17   Emily Stewart, "How the Republican Tax Cuts Are Failing Workers, in One Chart," Vox, July 23, 2018, https://www.vox.com/2018/7/23/17602746/tax-cuts-work-bloomberg-wages.

18   Meg Wiehe, Emanuel Nieves, Jeremie Greer and David Newville, *Race, Wealth and Taxes: How the Tax Cuts and Jobs Act Supercharges the Racial Wealth Divide* (Washington, DC: Institute on Taxation and Economic Policy, October 11, 2018), https://itep.org/race-wealth-and-taxes-how-the-tax-cuts-and-jobs-act-super charges-the-racial-wealth-divide/.

19   Manuel Madrid, "Think the GOP Tax Cut Was for the Rich? Actually, It Was for the White and Rich," *The American Prospect*, October 16, 2018, https://prospect.org/article/think-gop-tax-cut-was-rich-actually-it-was-white-and-rich.

20   Joshua Holland, "The GOP Tax Cuts Are Such a Blatant Scam That They Might Change the Whole Conversation," *Nation*, April 17, 2018, https://www.thenation.com/article/gop-tax-cuts-are-such-a-blatant-scam-that-they-might-change-the-whole-conversation/.

21   Senate Budget Committee, *Report: If Not for Republican Policies, the Federal Government Would Be Running a Surplus*, October 15,

2018, https://www.budget.senate.gov/ranking-member/news
room/press/report-if-not-for-republican-policies-the-federal
-government-would-be-running-a-surplus.

22   Nancy MacLean, introduction to *Democracy in Chains: The Deep
History of the Radical Right's Stealth Plan for America* (New York:
Penguin Books, 2017), xvii.

23   Bill Moyers, "The Great American Class War," Brennan Center
for Justice, December 12, 2013, https://www.brennancenter.org
/analysis/great-american-class-war.

24   Eric Levitz, "Inequality Is Rising Across the Globe—and
Skyrocketing in the U.S.," *New York Magazine*, December 15, 2017,
http://nymag.com/intelligencer/2017/12/inequality-is-rising
-globally-and-soaring-in-the-u-s.html?gtm=bottom.

25   Dave Lawler, "The Two Biggest Trends on Earth," Axios, August
6, 2018, https://www.axios.com/population-living-in-poverty
-around-the-world-4e9a1682-8635-46f5-8c20-43264b765c5e.html.

26   Michelle Goldberg, "The Debt-Shaming of Stacey Abrams," *New
York Times*, August 17, 2018, https://www.nytimes.com
/2018/08/17/opinion/columnists/stacey-abrams-georgia
-governor-debt.html.

CHAPTER 9

1   Dr. J. Marshall Shepherd, "What Is the National Climate
Assessment and Where Did It Come From?" *Forbes,* November
26, 2018, https://www.forbes.com/sites/marshall
shepherd/2018/11/26/what-is-the-national-climate-assessment
-and-where-did-it-come-from/#2b9620423666.

2   Penny Starr, "Experts on Climate Change Assessment: 'Every
Conclusion of This Latest Government Report Is False,'"

Breitbart News, November 25, 2018, https://www.breitbart.com/politics/2018/11/25/experts-climate-change-assessment-every-conclusion-latest-government-report-false/.

3   David Wallace-Wells, "UN Says Climate Genocide Is Coming. It's Actually Worse than That," *New York Magazine*, October 10, 2018, http://nymag.com/intelligencer/2018/10/un-says-climate-genocide-coming-but-its-worse-than-that.html.

4   Emily Atkin, "Al Gore's Carbon Footprint Doesn't Matter," *New Republic*, August 7, 2017, https://newrepublic.com/article/144199/al-gores-carbon-footprint-doesnt-matter.

5   "Scientific Consensus: Earth's Climate Is Warming," NASA, accessed January 9, 2019, https://climate.nasa.gov/scientific-consensus/.

6   "How Do We Know That Humans Are the Major Cause of Global Warming?" Union of Concerned Scientists, accessed January 9, 2019, https://www.ucsusa.org/how-do-we-know-humans-are-major-cause-global-warming#.XDaQTuJOk2x.

7   Dana Nuccitelli, "Here's What Happens When You Try to Replicate Climate Contrarian Papers," *Guardian*, August 25, 2015, https://www.theguardian.com/environment/climate-consensus-97-per-cent/2015/aug/25/heres-what-happens-when-you-try-to-replicate-climate-contrarian-papers.

8   "Koch Industries: Secretly Funding the Climate Denial Machine," Greenpeace, accessed January 9, 2019, https://www.greenpeace.org/usa/global-warming/climate-deniers/koch-industries/.

9   John Harwood, "Most Americans Want Action on Climate Change. Republicans Are the Exception: Poll," CNBC, December 17, 2018, https://www.cnbc.com/2018/12/17/americans-want-action-on-climate-change-republicans-are-the-exception-poll.html.

10   Cary Funk and Brian Kennedy, "Public Views on Climate Change and Climate Scientists," Pew Research Center, October 4, 2016, http://www.pewinternet.org/2016/10/04/public-views -on-climate-change-and-climate-scientists/.

11   C. J. Polychroniou, "Noam Chomsky: Moral Depravity Defines US Politics," Truthout, November 21, 2018, https://truthout.org /articles/noam-chomsky-moral-depravity-defines-us-politics/.

12   Juliet Eilperin and Brady Dennis, "How James Inhofe is Upending the Nation's Energy and Environmental Policies," *Washington Post,* March 14, 2017, https://www.washington post.com/national/health-science/how-james-inhofe-is -upending-the-nations-energy-and-environmental-policies/2017 /03/14/2bebdbfa-081c-11e7-a15f-a58d4a988474_story.html ?noredirect=on&utm_term=.12f069f80320.

13   Tom McKay, "What Science Says About the Senator Who Used a Snowball to 'Disprove' Climate Change," Mic, March 3, 2015, https://mic.com/articles/111666/here-s-what-science-has-to-say -about-sen-inhofe-s-ridiculous-climate-change-stunt#.egDO6Jjcv.

14   Kate Sheppard, "Mike Huckabee, Jim Inhofe Give How-To on Denying Climate Change Without Any Concern for Facts," HuffPost, August 19, 2013, https://www.huffingtonpost.com /2013/08/19/mike-huckabee-climate-change_n_3782300.html.

15   Brian Tashman, "Jim Inhofe: 'Our Kids Are Being Brainwashed' in School," Right Wing Watch, July 26, 2016, http://www.right wingwatch.org/post/jim-inhofe-our-kids-are-being-brain washed-in-school/.

16   Eilperin and Dennis, "How James Inhofe is Unpending the Nation's Energy and Environmental Policies," *Washington Post.*

17   Coral Davenport, "E.P.A. Chief Doubts Consensus View of Climate Change," *New York Times,* March 9, 2017, https://www

.nytimes.com/2017/03/09/us/politics/epa-scott-pruitt-global
-warming.html.

18   Joey Mendolia, "All of the Ways Scott Pruitt Changed Energy
      Policy," PBS, July 5, 2018, https://www.pbs.org/newshour
      /nation/all-of-the-ways-embattled-epa-chief-scott-pruitt
      -has-changed-energy-policy.

19   Jamelle Bouie, "Scott Pruitt's Legendary Corruption," *Slate*, July
      5, 2018, https://slate.com/news-and-politics/2018/07/scott
      -pruitt-was-allowed-to-perpetrate-a-staggering-level-of-self
      -dealing.html.

20   Patrick Smith, "Fed Up with New Direction Under Trump, EPA
      Staffers Exit the Agency," ThinkProgress, September 9, 2018,
      https://thinkprogress.org/epa-staffers-exodus-under-trump
      -8093c918f21f/.

21   Michael Barnard, "Male Right-Wing Nationalists Are Now
      All Climate Change Deniers," CleanTechnica, August 28, 2018,
      https://cleantechnica.com/2018/08/28/male-right-wing
      -nationalists-are-now-all-climate-change-deniers/.

22   Alex Seitz-Wald, "Why People Believe in Conspiracy Theories,"
      Salon, April 25, 2013, https://www.salon.com/2013/04/24/why
      _people_believe_in_conspiracy_theories/.

23   Jane Coaston, "#QAnon, the Scarily Popular Pro-Trump
      Conspiracy Theory, Explained," Vox, August 2, 2018, https:
      //www.vox.com/policy-and-politics/2018/8/1/17253444/qanon
      -trump-conspiracy-theory-reddit.

24   Molly Roberts, "QAnon is terrifying. This is why," *Washington
      Post*, August 2, 2018, https://www.washingtonpost.com/blogs
      /post-partisan/wp/2018/08/02/what-makes-qanon-so-scary
      /?utm_term=.5d300b232a4f.

25   Leah Payne and Brian Doak, "The Christian Conspiracies That
      Keep Evangelicals on Trump's Side," *Washington Post,* October 19,
      2018, https://www.washingtonpost.com/outlook/2018/10/19
      /christian-conspiracies-that-keep-evangelicals-trumps-side
      /?noredirect=on&utm_term=.da28od98024d.

26   Sharon Kelly, "'Time is Running Out,' American Petroleum
      Institute Chief Said in 1965 Speech on Climate Change,"
      DeSmogBlog (blog), November 20, 2018, https://www.desmog
      blog.com/2018/11/20/american-petroleum-institute-1965
      -speech-climate-change-oil-gas.

27   John Sutter and Lawrence Davidson, "Teen Tells Climate
      Negotiators They Aren't Mature Enough," CNN, December 17,
      2018, https://www.cnn.com/2018/12/16/world/greta-thunberg
      -cop24/index.html.

CONCLUSION

1   Kevin Baker, "BLUEXIT: A Modest Proposal for Separating Blue
      States from Red," *New Republic,* March 9, 2017, https://new
      republic.com/article/140948/bluexit-blue-states-exit-trump-red
      -america.

2   "Bluexit Proposal Would Separate Blue and Red States," *AM Joy,*
      MSNBC, July 2, 2017, https://www.msnbc.com/am-joy/watch
      /-bluexit-proposal-would-separate-blue-and-red-states
      -981891651779.

3   Van Jones, *Beyond the Messy Truth: How We Came Apart, How We
      Come Together* (New York: Ballentine Books, 2017), 192.

4   David Frum, "It's the Guns," *Atlantic,* May 18, 2018, https:/
      /www.theatlantic.com/ideas/archive/2018/05/its-the-
      guns/560771/.

5   Melissa Block, "2018 Brought a 'Tectonic Shift' in the Gun
     Control Movement, Advocates Say," NPR, December 26, 2018,
     https://www.npr.org/2018/12/26/678248648/2018-brought-a
     -tectonic-shift-in-the-gun-control-movement-advocates-say.

6   Sherrilyn Ifill (@Sifill_LDF), "When you lose, it's someone
     else's turn. But what we're seeing now increasingly is an
     effort to rig the game to ensure that one side never loses. The
     permanent . . .," Twitter, December 1, 2018, https://twitter.com
     /Sifill_LDF/status/1068888762191630336.

7   Ari Berman, "Democrats' First Order of Business: Making
     It Easier to Vote and Harder to Buy Elections," *Mother Jones,*
     January 4, 2019, https://www.motherjones.com/politics/2019/01
     /democrats-first-order-of-business-making-it-easier-to-vote-and
     -harder-to-buy-elections/.

8   Roxane Gay, "Indiana Is Not Protecting Religious Freedom But
     Outright Zealotry," *Guardian,* March 27, 2015, https://www
     .theguardian.com/commentisfree/2015/mar/27/ndiana-is-not
     -protecting-religious-freedom-but-outright-zealotry?CMP
     =edit_2221.

9   Carroll Doherty, "Key Findings on Americans' Views of the
     U.S. Political System and Democracy," Pew Research Center,
     April 26, 2018, http://www.pewresearch.org/fact-tank
     /2018/04/26/key-findings-on-americans-views-of-the-u-s
     -political-system-and-democracy/.

10   Thomas E. Mann, "Admit It, Political Scientists: Politics Really Is
     More Broken Than Ever," *Atlantic,* May 26, 2014, https://www
     .theatlantic.com/politics/archive/2014/05/dysfunction/371544/.

ACKNOWLEDGMENTS

This book is inspired by the principled digital warriors I've engaged, debated, battled, and befriended since I first entered the political arena in 2001. Their dedication to truth and justice keeps our democracy alive.

I'm grateful to the following individuals for opening doors that made my career in politics—and this book—possible: Karen Kohn Bradley, Richard Bell, Chris Heinz, Joan Walsh, James Boyce, Howard Wolfson, and Patti Solis Doyle.

John Kerry and Hillary Clinton gave me a front row seat to history and I will always be honored to have represented them on the digital battlefield.

I owe a big debt of gratitude to the Melville House team: Dennis, Valerie, Ryan, Tim, Stephanie, et al., for their guidance and vision.

I am deeply grateful to my friends and family, who have shared my improbable journey from Beirut war survivor to music producer to presidential campaign adviser—and now to author.

I thank Robert, Michael, and Seth for their commitment and friendship over the years.

Thank you especially to my wife Leela, for her many hours of research, her invaluable insights, her unwavering support, her dedication to the creative process, and for braving the maelstrom of social media with me. She is my better half in every way.

INDEX